PIZZ&
LO&E

Legendary pepperoni cupping
at Prince St. Pizza, NYC.

HISTORY · RECIPES · STORIES

PIZZA

PEOPLE · PLACES · LOVE

A BOOK BY PIZZA PILGRIMS

DESIGN & PHOTOGRAPHY BY DAVE BROWN

Hardie Grant

QUADRILLE

James on the oven at BST
festival in Hyde Park in 2019.

Contents

Introduction

This is our pizza magnum opus.

Ever since we embarked on our 'Pizza Pilgrimage' in October 2011 we have
wanted to write a book about pizza. In all the 8 years (and counting) that
have passed since (of which we have spent every waking minute thinking
about pizza), this feeling has only got stronger.

'We all know someone who LOVES pizza – and we mean *really* loves it.'

The fact is that pizza is special. There is something about the combination
of dough, cheese and tomatoes – plus the fact that pizza is round, eaten
with your hands and therefore made for sharing – that makes humanity and
their bellies gravitate towards it. Or, since the invention of home delivery,
makes the pizza gravitate towards *us*. Think about it for a minute. We all
know someone who LOVES pizza – and we mean *really* loves it. Someone
who identifies themselves by their love of pizza, be it with a badge, T-shirt,
notebook, or twitter handle.

And in contrast, can you think of anyone you know who hates pizza? Not
someone who is gluten-intolerant (as they quite often identify that condition
with the singular truth that pizza is now off limits and they are distraught),
but a true pizza despiser. We bet you can't think of a single person.

A little investigation on the internet backs up our simple theory that pizza
makes people happy. Not in an 'I am hungry and I need food' kind of way. Not
in an 'it's just convenient' kind of way. It's much deeper than that. Google is
awash with people talking about pizza as the only dependable thing in their
lives; something that compares with their spouse, their best friend or their
family in a way that tacos, ribs or burgers never could. Pizza is special.

Once you start to work with the product itself you begin to see the
reasoning behind this. We now have numerous pizzerias across London and
have been working with Neapolitan pizza chefs for almost a decade. Every
single chef we meet has a connection with pizza at a fundamental level,
and even the ones who have been doing it for many, many years still see
themselves as students. There is always something new to learn, something

new to try and something new to teach. It's the full *Othello* – takes a moment to understand but a lifetime to master. Write off pizza as a simple dish at your own peril.

Pizza is a food designed for sharing – you use your hands, you swap slices and its very roundness makes it more approachable (King Arthur was really on to something). Sharing a pizza with a mate, or a date, or your mum is just special. And you just know that if the feeding of the 5,000 happened in the 21st century the big man would turn to pizza as his best option.

It cannot be an accident that almost every culture on earth has (in many cases, independently) adopted, created or borrowed a form of pizza that is central to its cuisine.

Pizza is also central to so many cultural touch points: from movies, to books, to television and even sports. Whether via online videos, corporate sponsorship, character development or plot point, pizza permeates them all.

We wanted to write a book to capture all of this in one heavenly place. To celebrate pizza in all forms and document its cultural significance. It has been an amazing project, one with endless roads and a bottomless pit of pizza discoveries – the more we think about it, the more ideas come to light. So, this is our attempt to honour the pizza. Our *A Brief History of Pizza*. Our *Hitchhikers Guide to Pizza*. Our *Principia Pizzatica*. It is packed with incredible info, from pizza world records and pizza city guides to all of our Pizza Pilgrims recipes. Most importantly, it is full of all of the amazing people from around the world who have dedicated their lives to pizza. Without them, pizza is nothing.

We set off on our Pizza Pilgrimage in our three-wheeled van in 2011. What we are fast beginning to realise is that a pizza pilgrimage never ever ends...

Pizza is a totally subjective medium – everyone has their own favourites, recommendations and opinions! Let us know what we have missed at pizzabook@pizzapilgrims.co.uk.

THE PIZZA PILGRIM

Everyone loves pizza!
no one is doing it yet!
WE SHOULD BUY
A PIAGGIO APE VAN →
AND PUT A PIZZA OVEN IN IT!
WE SHOULD DEFO
BUY A VAN IN ITALY
AND DRIVE IT BACK!

PIZZA

ape

A long(ish) time ago, in country quite far away...

The Pizza Pilgrimage, the place where it all started for us, began fairly inauspiciously. Turns out, a £3.50 pizza on the Ryan Air flight from Stansted Airport was never going to be the finest exponent of over 200 years of pizza history. It was, however, our start line, and we still ate the whole thing (highlighting one of the endearing pizza truths – it always tastes pretty good whatever the circumstances!).

Only a few months before, we had decided to undertake a trip the length of Italy in search of pizza perfection. Over a few beers in London's Shepherd's Bush we bemoaned our 'proper' jobs and how we just wanted to find a way to get into food. The explosion of street food in London had given us an opportunity, and now we just needed to climb the hurdle of knowing nothing about how to run a food business.

One beer became two. Maybe we should focus on pizza, given everyone loves pizza and no one is doing it yet? Three beers. Maybe we should buy a Piaggio Ape van and put a pizza oven in the back? Four beers. We should definitely buy the van in Italy, and drive it back on an exploratory pizza trip to save us some money on import duty. And thus, the Pizza Pilgrimage was born. The next day, slightly hungover, we started planning...

IAGE

The Van

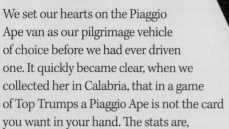

We set our hearts on the Piaggio Ape van as our pilgrimage vehicle of choice before we had ever driven one. It quickly became clear, when we collected her in Calabria, that in a game of Top Trumps a Piaggio Ape is not the card you want in your hand. The stats are, in a word, woeful.

We think the only technical attribute the van wins at is turning in a circle. That said, drive one and everything melts away. It's just immediately endearing – like driving a toy car – and also a flashback to trying to start a dodgy car in the mid-nineties, carefully using just the right amount of revs and choke…

The performance is definitely an issue. The van is *so* slow that what was planned as a week-long trip took almost six weeks, not least as we only discovered on arrival that Apes are not allowed on the *autostrada*. On some of the larger hills we were genuinely concerned that we would not make it. We have footage of us being overtaken up one hill by a jogger – always a low point in a motorised vehicle. And we once turned a corner too vigorously, taking her onto two wheels (*Police Academy*-style). Then, to top it all off, we almost tipped her onto her back when trying to leave a multi-storey car park at speed…

But the Ape (Italian for 'bee', the worker version of the Vespa, which in turn means 'wasp') is true to its mission. It is a grafter; designed to rebuild Italy after World War II. And eight years after Piaggio told us, categorically, that she could not carry a 1-tonne pizza oven, she is still driving from event to event in London without complaining. Much.

1D

Piaggio Ape

Top Speed	30 mph
Top Speed Uphill	10 mph
Engine Size	219 cc
Wheels	3
Gears	4
0-60 mph	Never

GENOA, HOME OF: BASIL
The often unsung pizza ingredient (especially by Thom's five-year-old who hates anything green on his pizza) – basil has its home in Genoa. Basil not only holds a regal place as one of the four toppings on a Margherita, it is also the key ingredient in pesto, which forms the base for many a pizza around the world.
During our visit we met with the world pesto champion(!), who also happens to grow basil in massive greenhouses, to learn a thing or two *about this aromatic delight.*

TUSCANY, HOME OF: OLIVE OIL
OK, so, olive oil comes from all over Italy, but our first experience of its production took place just outside Pisa in Tuscany.
Truly fresh, first pressing olive oil is unlike anything you'll find in the supermarket. It is bright green, thick like crude oil and has a massively peppery, fresh taste. The first time we tried it we could not stop coughing (see YouTube for proof). But, as with so many Italian ingredients, it is a thing of beauty – and elevates pizza to another dimension.

REGGIO EMILIA, HOME OF: PARMESAN
Parmesan is the secret ingredient on almost all great pizzas, adding a layer of umami complexity (how legit does that sound) to every pizza. It is truly an amazing product and learning how it develops over three years of maturation (during which time a warehouse can house tens of millions of euros' worth of stock) was a real education.

PARMA, HOME OF: CURED MEAT
You say Parma, we say ham! Actually, so do most people come to think of it. Still the king of cured meats, seeing Parma ham being produced was a real highlight of the trip – and tasting it on pizza tells you it is *worth all the effort.*

ROME, HOME OF: MORE PIZZA!
The other heavy hitter of the Italian pizza map, Rome is probably less obsessed with pizza than Naples. That said, it has two distinct varieties of its own, and still definitely ranks in the top five best pizza cities on the planet. More on that later!

The Plan

④ **LAZIO, HOME OF: TIELLA** Home to Rome, Lazio has an important part to play in Italy's pizza story. One of our favourite discoveries there was our encounter with tiella in a small port town called Gaeta. Tiella is halfway between a pie and a pizza and is usually filled with the local catch of the day (and eaten once the pubs close). Delicious.

③ **NAPLES, HOME OF: PIZZA!** Deserving of a special mention, Naples is the Asgard of pizza. It's where it all started and pizza is still revered in the city, almost as much as Diego Maradona and the towering Vesuvio. Pizza is an art form in Naples and, when it comes down to it, this book is basically just an homage to this city. It is a mad, brilliant, emotional, exuberant, amazing place and, if you haven't been, you need to get on the next flight. It is also pretty telling that the Caputo flour mill – home of the world's best pizza flour – has its home in Naples. *'Nuff said.*

② **CAMPAGNIA, HOME OF: TOMATOES / MOZZARELLA** Campania is the home of Naples, which is in turn the home of pizza. In terms of your standard pizza pilgrimage, this is the Holy Grail of regions, providing the amazing ingredients that form the basis of the best pizza on the planet. From tomatoes grown in the foothills of Mount Vesuvius to buffalo mozzarella made fresh and eaten warm, Campania is a must-visit for anyone wanting to understand the complexities of the world's greatest foodstuff.

① **CALABRIA, HOME OF: 'NDUJA** Our starting point for the trip and the place where we first sat behind the wheel of our Ape van. Aside from this fateful meeting, we also discovered 'nduja here – a mega hit of meaty, chilli flavour. We think we may have been among the first people to use it as a pizza topping on our return to the UK, but now you can find it everywhere (great news, because it's *delicious*).

＊ See the following pages for photos from the pilgrimage!

We set off to Italy with two missions. One was fairly dishonourable
– to save money on the import tax on the vehicle. The second was
more romantic – to learn everything that Italy knew about pizza, from
the tip of her toe to the top of her thigh. We will let this book be the
answer as to whether we achieved the latter, but let us just say that,
between us, we put on almost 3 stone trying... The space in the cab
of the Ape was significantly cosier by the end of the trip.

We set out with a map of Italy, pin-pointed with the key places we
wanted to visit. Basically, we were on a mission to travel anywhere
that had even the remotest connection with pizza. Inevitably, in Italy,
that meant a fair few stops. Here are some of the highlights...

PIZZA PILGRIMS BIG FIGHT PROMOTIONS LTD PRESENTS

A SENSATIONAL HEAVYWEIGHT CONTEST

IN THE BLUE CORNER

HOME OF PIZZA AND STILL THE UNDISPUTED CHAMPION AFTER 200 YEARS

NAPLES
VS
ROME

IN THE RED CORNER

ROME IS A BIT OF A CHEAT AS IT HAS TWO CONTENDERS IN THE RING

FIRST, THE CELEBRATION OF COLOUR AND FLAVOUR THAT IS PIZZA AL TAGLIO (SEE PAGE 60)

SECOND, THE WAFER-THIN PIZZA THAT REPRESENTS SIMPLICITY ITSELF

OBVIOUSLY, THIS PARTICULAR BATTLE HAS BEEN GOING ON FOR DECADES, AND THE JUDGES' SCORECARDS NEVER SEEM TO AGREE

BUT, IF YOU ASK US (AND IT IS OUR BOOK AFTER ALL) NAPLES WINS BY A KNOCK OUT IN THE FIRST ROUND

Neapolitan Pizza: Our home from home

Naples is a city that grabs your attention from the off – most likely as you pull out of the airport in a taxi and immediately have your life flash before your eyes. It is a mad, melting pot of a city, bursting with vibrancy and energy, exactly what you might expect from a city built at the base of an active volcano that has already buried Pompeii and is overdue a second crack of the whip...

But the thing you will always remember about Naples is the pizza. It is, in a word, sublime. We had eaten pizza all our lives, but the second we tried pizza in Naples, true Neapolitan pizza, there was nothing else for us.

It really is all about balance. From the light, doughy crust to the sweet tomatoes, to the milky, acidic fior di latte mozzarella and aromatic basil. A perfect Neapolitan Margherita really is a masterpiece – even Da Vinci would be chuffed with it. There is a reason why it is protected by UNESCO and comes with a casual 27-page guide from the AVPN (Naples Pizza Police) on how to make it.

We can't give you sound advice on praying, or loving for that matter, but if you are looking for good eating, you would do worse than Julia Roberts' choice of a Neapolitan pizza! We now go back to Naples at least three times every year and are still totally in love with the place. Check out our Naples city guide on page 46 for our favourite locations for pizza, in the city where it all began.

Another team Pilgrimage to Naples.

Dough making with Ciro Oliva.

€1 spritz at Cammarota in the Spanish quarter.

Our album cover...

After the Pilgrimage

'We drove the van to Soho in London and set up a little market stall on Berwick Street, working five days a week selling pizza (and improving our technique with every day that went by).'

Once we returned from our epic pilgrimage through Italy, the hard work really started. James headed back to Naples to work in a Neapolitan pizzeria and get to the heart of how to make amazing pizza dough (see page 100). Thom set off to (the significantly more glamorous) Colchester, back in the UK, to start work on fitting our amazing, domed Pavesi pizza oven into the Ape (it wasn't quite as easy as we thought it might be!).

Once the oven was in place, we were ready to unleash our pizza onto the unsuspecting British public. We drove the van to Soho in London and set up a little market stall on Berwick Street, working five days a week selling pizza (and improving our technique with every day that went by). We attended festivals across the country, we made pizza in the sunshine, rain, hail and snow, and we learned a great deal about what works and what does not.

After 18 months, we got the opportunity to open our own pizzeria, and are now lucky enough to have a quite a few more dotted across London and the UK. We are still learning little tips, tricks and leg-ups to make better pizza every single day but, the truth is, the Neapolitans are 100% right – you can make pizza your whole life and you'll still only ever be a student!

Pizza Pilgrims in the
City of London.

The History of Pizza

'The US alone consumes three billion pizzas a year.'

Pizza is the world's favourite fast food (and thus the world's favourite food). An indication of the scale we are talking about – the US alone consumes three billion pizzas a year.

That's over nine pizzas for every single person who lives there. We don't know how many times around the world they would stretch, but you get the idea: **pizza is a big deal.**

Aligning with the global reach of pizza today, it is fitting that its origins are equally global. While Italy has, no doubt, a very strong claim to having done more for pizza than any other nation, the various elements that make up a pizza, as we know it today, have been influenced by millennia of culinary history. Here is our effort at unpicking what is a surprisingly half-baked historical backdrop for the humble pizza...

THE FİRST QUESTİON YOU REALLY HAVE TO ASK YOURSELF İS: WHAT MAKES A PİZZA, A PİZZA?

You could take the position that any flatbread with toppings is a pizza. If that's the case, then pizza is OLD. We mean seriously old. The first claimed existence of pizza seems to be in Neolithic times, which technically ended in 4500 BC. If we are honest, though, we can't really find anything concrete to back this up.

This was, allegedly, the first time that we humans ground wheat to make flour and then cooked it. While this is technically a version of unleavened bread, it's probably taking a bit of leap to say this was the first occurrence of pizza. More solid evidence starts to emerge around 30 BC, where something that could totally actually be pizza appears in no less than Virgil's classic poem the *Aeneid*. Written between 29 BC and 19 BC, the poem describes the hero Aeneas arriving with his crew in Latium and sitting down to enjoy a meal of 'thin wheaten cakes' used as plates topped with mushrooms and herbs. 'Look! We have eaten our plates!' exclaim his well-fed group – the poem potentially touching on lack of washing up as one of the main drivers for the success of pizza in modern times. Obviously, this means that pizza may technically have existed when Jesus was doing his thing. There is also plenty of evidence of 'topped flatbreads' appearing in ancient Egyptian (*fiteer*), Greek (*pitta*) and Roman (*panis focacius*) cuisine, not to mention the Babylonians. However, if you look at most definitions of pizza (i.e. a large circle of flatbread baked with cheese, tomatoes, and sometimes meat and vegetables spread on top), then tomato and cheese are essential additions to make pizza, well, pizza. This comes with some challenges (e.g. is a modern Marinara not a pizza?). However, in a *Family Fortunes*-style survey, we are adamant that 'cheese' and 'tomato' would top any list of likely things to find on your pizza. As such, we are going to base most of our history lesson from the point that this became true.

'Look! We have even eaten our plates!'

Naples and the Early Forms of Neapolitan Pizza

Naples is undoubtedly the birthplace of modern pizza and, notwithstanding the definition of pizza agreed above, the final resting place of pizza does have its origins in a more basic version.

When Naples became a republic in the late 18th century, the population exploded. Unfortunately, this left a lot of people living in abject poverty as the city's infrastructure could not keep up. Known as the *lazzaroni*, allegedly due to their resemblance to Lazarus, these poor souls moved from pillar to post looking for any work they could get their hands on. This led to the requirement for a food that was not only cheap but also easy to eat on the move. Pizza: enter stage right. It was the original *cucina povera* (peasant cooking), born out of necessity for people who could not afford the luxuries of the rich. Fact is, some of the world's favourite dishes today are born from the same movement: necessity is the mother of invention.

The early versions were simplicity itself, topped with garlic, lard and salt. Additional combinations were soon fallen upon; although, unexpectedly, the first 'cheese' that made its way onto pizza was made from horse milk. Toppings also included baby fish (likely anchovies) and even basil in some cases. These pizzas were sold from street stalls, rather than pizzerias, and were very quickly denigrated as 'vile food' only fit for the poor, unwashed *lazzaroni*. Obviously, if people actually had bothered to taste it, they may have been less quick to knock it.

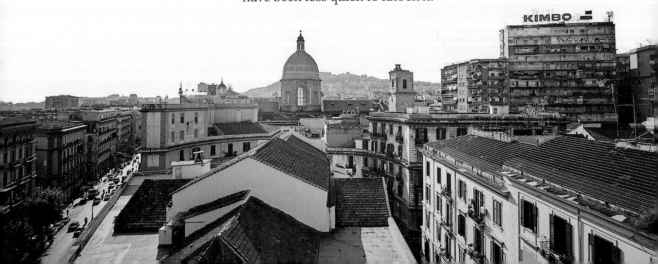

The Word 'Pizza'

Pizza directly translates as 'pie' in modern Italian, and is probably about as international a word as 'hello' or 'OK'. As usual, there is not exactly a consensus here as to precisely where the word originates (etymologists are at a bit of a loss), but here are a few little factoids and potential origin stories for you to ponder over. It's probably best if you make your own mind up about which one you want to tell your mates about down the pub...

PITA - The Greek word for 'flatbread', and friend of hummus lovers everywhere, this could be how pizza came to be. Naples was originally founded by the Greeks, so the story checks out.

PIX/PICEA - Of Latin origin, this literally means 'of pitch'. This is a term which may refer to the texture, appearance and colour of baked bread. If you think of the charred areas on a modern Neapolitan pizza this starts to make a little more sense.

BIZZO - From a West Germanic language, this is the Langobardic word for 'bite'. A complicated geo-political history around the time of the invention of pizza makes this a possible contender.

PIZZICARE - Literally meaning 'to pinch' in Italian. The theory is that, as you have to pinch the dough to make a flatbread, this could be how the word for pizza was born. Seems unlikely to us, but what do we know?

PINSA - Another Latin word for flatbread, derived from the word for 'clamp'. We have searched hard for a reason why this might be connected to the modern-day pizza, but have come up short. Incidentally, whilst almost everyone you ask would tell you that pizza started on the streets of Naples, evidence has been recently found that the first mention of the actual word 'pizza' was in the port town of Gaeta about 80 miles north. Obviously, this is just the first written mention of it, but it adds a little spice to the concrete version of events that

PIZZA

originated in
Naples.

The 24-hour street bars on the seafront in Naples that *never* close.

KILLER TOMATOES

As usual, the debate rages as to when tomatoes first made their appearance on pizza. We delve more into the topic of tomatoes on page 62, but it is worth mentioning here how they ended up on pizza in the first place.

Tomatoes first arrived in Europe from South America with the Spanish Conquistadors. Why they brought them over is really a total mystery, as they were initially thought to be poisonous (partly due to their close relation the nightshade family, and partly because they were originally eaten from pewter plates, which tended to give the eater lead poisoning!). Reminds us of the classic 1978 vegetable comedy horror movie *Attack of the Killer Tomatoes*. No, we're not joking – check it out!

Anyway, tomatoes arrived in Europe, and then spent 200 years only being grown for ornamental purposes. These 'golden apples' (literally the direct translation of the word *pomodoro*; to this day the word for tomato in modern Italian) would originally have been yellow in colour and clearly weren't trusted. It is for that very reason that the poor downtrodden of Naples started putting them on pizza. They were not in demand, so were very cheap to buy, and the locals also noticed that wild animals ate them without any ill effects.

Thus, in the early 18th century, pizzas started appearing with tomatoes on them – and it's fair to say we haven't looked back since.

BUFFALO MOZZARELLA

Mozzarella or, to use its full name, *Mozzarella di Bufala Campana*, is actually made from buffalo milk and has been produced in some form or other in the Campania region (whose capital is Naples) since the 16th century. A similar cheese, known as *mozza*, was actually produced by monks in the same region, but from cows' milk, as early as the 12th century. Why, then, did production switch to buffalo milk – and buffalo end up in Italy in the first place?!

The story goes that buffalo were introduced to Sicily by Arabic conquerors of the island in AD 827. These conquerors had a huge impact on Sicilian agriculture (maybe due to similar arid conditions). When they were in turn conquered (why do people not use this word so much now?) by the Normans and pushed to the mainland, they subsequently brought buffalo over the water to Campania and Naples.

Buffalo milk has a much higher fat content than cows' milk, which leads to the extremely rich, creamy texture of buffalo mozzarella (see more on page 64). That said, cows' milk mozzarella is still a local staple, and was actually a necessity when, after World War II, the retreating German armies slaughtered all the buffalo in southern Italy. During this period, mozzarella production had to switch to cows' milk for a few years while buffalo populations were replenished.

From those early, local makers in Campania in the 16th century, mozzarella production just grew and grew – most likely because it is bloody delicious. Word of mouth always wins through. The real conspiracy theory is why it took almost 100 years for someone to figure out that mozzarella could work well on a pizza…

The Margherita

Here it is. The real moment when pizza as we know it was born.

Every pizzeria in Naples will likely tell you that they had a hand in inventing the Margherita. It is, however, clearly Pizzeria Brandi, the restaurant near Plaza di Plebiscito in Naples, that have the proof to back up the claims.

It was here, in 1889, that the most famous pizza chef in Naples, Raffaele Esposito, was given the task of cooking for King Umberto I and his wife Margherita, the Queen of Savoy. The story goes that the royal couple were tired of the rich, over-the-top French cuisine that the upper classes were subject to morning, noon and night (tough life!) and they were looking for something more basic to enjoy on their visit to Naples. Raffaele stepped up, and made them three varieties of the local delicacy: pizza. The final of the three pizzas was topped with mozzarella, tomato sauce and fresh basil, allegedly to signify the colours of the early version of the Italian flag.

Preserved to this day, Pizzeria Brandi still have the letter from Queen Margherita herself declaring this final offering was 'found to be delicious'. The dish was instantly named Pizza Margherita in her honour – a name that clearly stuck. ('Esposito' is still a very famous name in the Neapolitan pizza scene and, actually, our first taste of Neapolitan pizza came courtesy of one Antonino Esposito, a celebrity pizza chef in Italy.)

Pizza culture grew from there, with new topping combinations entering the scene slowly but surely. However, it is the Margherita that has remained the truest articulation of what pizza is all about.

It is now protected by UNESCO as a world heritage food, and it is still by far the best seller in all of our pizzerias.

In fact, one of the most famous pizzerias in Naples, Da Michele, still only sell a Margherita and a Marinara pizza. For how to make a delicious Neapolitan Margherita, turn to our recipe on page 104.

Enter the

Interestingly, despite royal approval, pizza still remained a relatively local staple in Naples for the next few decades. It was, surprisingly, the Americans who actually caused pizza to be more well known throughout Italy, and who gave pizza its synonymous nature with the country of its invention.

'It took the involvement of America to bring pizza to the masses.'

In the late 19th century, Neapolitans starting emigrating to the New World in search of work. And, once they got there, they of course missed pizza (who wouldn't?).

The first American pizzeria of note, Lombardi's (see page 214), opened in 1905 with a coal-fired oven and a distinctly New York take on the Neapolitan classic (amazingly, it still has the original oven!). From this historic point forward, pizza was positioned as a fast, fun, cheap and accessible food, and its popularity exploded across America. Variants abounded (more on this later), and bemused Neapolitan immigrants grew increasingly confused with the plethora of things Americans would do with pizza (for example, for a country that took 100 years to put mozzarella on pizza, the invention of the Chicago Deep Dish in 1948 was a big leap).

When World War II broke out, Europe was awash with American troops. Along with blue jeans and rock 'n' roll, the Americans also brought the idea of pizza to the far reaches of Italy. It was from here that a national popularity of pizza abounded. Despite the unification of Italy under one flag in 1946 – and as with so many things – it took the involvement of America to bring pizza to the masses.

Pizza Hangover.
Post-Pizza Expo in Vegas, 2017.

US Pizzerias of Note

TONY'S PIZZA NAPOLETANA – LA

Tony Gemignani is as close to a legend of pizza as you could imagine (13 times pizza world champion, innit), so it goes without saying that his flagship pizza place in Los Angeles is a shrine to pizza. Like a true 'collector', what makes this place really special is that it celebrates within its four walls the full gamut of pizza varieties from across Italy and the US. So, you can sit at the same table and order a Neapolitan wood-fired pizza, a gas-fired grandma slice and an electric-cooked Romana pizza! As an operation it makes our eyes water, but it really has to be seen to be believed. One thing is clear, as Tony would say, this place totally 'respects the craft' and is a great place to go on a tour of pizza history and style without leaving your table. Just remember: no reservations, no exceptions – be ready to wait! See our interview with Tony on page 250.

PIZZA ROCK

We know, you can spot a pattern emerging here. So, this second pizzeria on this list belongs to... drum roll please... Tony Gemignani (did we mention the 13 times he was World Pizza Champion?). This place has all the pizza creds that Tony's Pizza Napoletana has but, being in Las Vegas, it brings the party vibe, with DJs, an excessive craft beer list and cocktails (and dreamz). It was created in partnership with George Karpaty and Trevor Hewitt (of Ruby Skye San Francisco fame), so nightclub energy runs through the place. Good times guaranteed.

PIZZA BRAIN

Pizza Brain is a true labour of love. It is both a pizzeria and a museum of pizza culture; the latter being home to a Guinness-World-Record-winning collection of pizza memorabilia from the US. And it really is an amazing celebration of all things pizza in America. It is the vibe of the place that is really unique though, with a focus on community and a home-spun feel (one of the co-founders, it turns out, is an amateur carpenter and was let loose on the interiors – to charming effect!).

It is important that this place is not seen as a novelty – the pizza is serious business, with locally sourced ingredients and awards left, right and centre. It is a real cultural landmark for pizza, and happens to be in Philadelphia, rather than in Chicago or New York!

EVEL PIE

God bless Las Vegas. People really know how to turn it up to 11 there! In their infinite wisdom, the great people of Sin City realised that the world was missing something – and that was a fusion of Evel Knievel and Pizza. And, god damn it, they were right! This is an ode to Evel's famous attempt to jump the Caesar's Palace fountains, but (obviously) through the medium of pizza. It is shameless and totally brilliant. Fantastic New York-style pizza in a psychotic nightmare of leather, motorbikes and flaming wall art. It is totally bonkers, and not to be missed (not least as it gets you 'off strip' so you can stop feeling like you're in *The Matrix* for 5 minutes). **Live hard, ride fast, eat pizza.**

PIZZERIA BIANCO

Chris Bianco did the unthinkable – he left his native New York to start a pizzeria in Phoenix, Arizona, no less. And what a pizzeria it is.

Lauded by almost every critic who has lifted a pen, he is the only pizza chef to win a regional James Beard award. Pizzeria Bianco still keeps it real and the menu is simple and classic, using local wheat flour and even making their own mozzarella on-site everyday. In his own words, 'it is all about balance', which is evident in all the pies on offer here.

Chris himself has now hung up his peel – years of making every single pie wreaked havoc on his asthma – but the pies are still some of the best in the US of A.

CHUCK E. CHEESE

We just couldn't do a pizza book without mentioning Chuck E. Cheese, the world famous pizzeria video game arcade with a mouse as their mascot.

The inspiration behind Pizza Planet in *Toy Story*, Chuck E. Cheese was actually founded by the same guy that started Atari in the '70s. We'll be honest, it won't be the best pizza you'll ever eat, but it is a part of US pizza history, so try and dodge the kids' parties and check it out when you can.

Right: Louis, the legendary owner of Sam's in Brooklyn. Great taste in pizza *and* t-shirts.

The Best Fictional Pizzerias

Amazing pizzerias you can never visit

Movies and TV shows are littered with depictions of pizzerias across America, reflecting the role that pizza has to play in American culture. And, in turn, it has influenced our view of what a pizzeria is about. The focus here is rarely on the pizza, but more on the role of a pizzeria as a place for people to come together, spend time with family and maybe even shed a tear or two.

HOME ALONE – LİTTLE NERO'S

Home Alone is almost as much a film about pizza as it is about Kevin. Pizza is pretty much the reason he is left at home in the first place (10 large pizzas ordered for four adults and 11 kids will probably cause you to sleep in).

We never actually get to see the inside of Little Nero's pizzeria, but we feel like we would love it. It is clearly quirky (the sign on the delivery car says, slightly oddly, 'No fiddlin' around', with a picture of a little man with a violin) and the staff are polite, if busy – the statue always gets picked up when they knock it over.

We are assuming that the name is a rip-off of the iconic pizza place Little Caesars, but that is never confirmed. What is clear is that Little Nero's plays a part in probably the most famous pizza scene in cinema history... (see page 226).

TOY STORY – PİZZA PLANET

So, this is obviously a rip-off of Chuck E. Cheese, the legendary pizzeria and kids' party venue that took America by storm. That said, it is probably one of the most well-realised and well-thought-out 'concept' pizzerias to ever exist in the movies. It plays a central role in the first *Toy Story* movie, as well as the origin story for one of the most iconic characters – the little green aliens. However, what really hammers home how much the guys at Pixar love Pizza Planet (and we are going to have to hazard a guess that they enjoyed a pizza or two while doing all that animating) is that there is a nod to PP in every Pixar movie to date (with the bizarre exception of *The Incredibles*).

Despite the header to this section, mega fans can actually visit a version of Pizza Planet (called the bizarrely similar Alien's Pizza Planet) at the Tomorrowland section of Disney theme parks.

DO THE RİGHT THİNG – SAL'S FAMOUS PİZZERİA

Sal's pizzeria sits at the heart of this, one of the best films ever made. The pizzeria forms the backdrop for the action and is at the centre of the racial tension of a Brooklyn neighbourhood transitioning from traditionally Italian-American to African-American. The apex of this challenge is represented through a motif famous in pizzerias across the world – the wall of 'celebrities'. It is fair to say that Sal's has done more to ingrain the image of a New York pizzeria in popular culture than almost any other.

FUTURAMA – FAMILY BROS PIZZERIA

An obvious tip of the hat to the family-run nature of pizzerias in the States (with the family name often making the signage), we are guessing that this is one pizzeria you would never want to visit.

Found in New York, it is run by an alien race, the Cygnoids, who are famed for their lack of knowledge on how to cook, and what humans want from life. This leads to an odd selection of pizza toppings including silt, asbestos, flaming magnesium, stucco, scarab, and guano (which any study of *Ace Ventura II* will tell you is bat droppings). And to drink? How about some wine made from crushed rats…

MYSTIC PIZZA

Mystic Pizza is the only movie we can think of the where the pizzeria is the title of the movie itself. What we love about it is that it is the epitome of a family-run pizza joint – something that is close to our hearts!

The most brilliant scene is undoubtedly when the posh food critic comes to visit. It perfectly recreates the feeling of having a critic inside your own restaurant – a combination of excitement, nerves and dread. It is such a great moment when he gives them the one-word review – 'Superb!'. But our favourite part, the one that really sums it all up, is when he notes that he can't quite put his finger on all the spices and herbs in their sauce, to which the chef shouts 'Damn right you can't!' – the perfect summation of every pizzeria owner in history.

BILLIONS – CAPPARELLO'S PIZZERIA

You know when a pizza works for a billionaire as picky as Bobby Axelrod that it must be good pizza. And you can tell from one look at Capparello's that the pizza really is the only reason to go there.

We love so many things about Capparello's; from the amazing long-term owner, to the fact they serve wine in tumblers (like we do!). But what we love most about it is what it says about pizza in a more general sense.

This is Bobby Axelrod's 'Rosebud' replacement – the place that reminds him where he came from and where he goes for comfort in the tough times. It is also the place he goes to make a point – showing that keeping up standards, against all odds and over the long term, is the real way to business success. So, hats off to Capparello's and its iconic Nonna slice – the cornerstone of family business in NYC for centuries!

L'ORO DI NAPOLI

The film is an ode to Naples from 1955, featuring none other than Sophia Loren as a pizza maker extraordinaire.

The film is a perfect encapsulation of the kind of pizzeria most likely frequented by true inhabitants of Napoli (unlike some of the places that have more of a touristy focus on the Via dei Tribunali). True, the pizza they serve is pizza fritta – made with a steaming vat of oil for cooking rather than a proper pizza oven (see page 54) – but the vibe is bang on. Naples is still packed with streetside pizzerias like this, where for three euros you can buy a perfect Margherita for eating at home or on the go. The basket delivery method, shown for getting pizza to the apartment above, has now, inevitably, been replaced by swarms of Vespa drivers – some driving with stacks of ten pizzas balanced on one hand while steering with the other. But the feeling of the place is just perfect Naples. As is Sophia Loren.

Pizza of the World

There must be something universally appealing about a flatbread topped with great ingredients and baked, so much so that it seems almost every culture has their own twist on the dish. *The Oxford English Dictionary* calls a pizza 'a flat, round base of dough baked with a topping of tomatoes, cheese, onions etc.' Well, we think we can chuck that definition out the window as the original pizza Marinara has *no* cheese. So, with nothing tying us down, we're going to make our own definition up and stick it in *The Pizza Pilgrim's Dictionary*:

Pizza [peet-suh]
noun
1. A pizza has a base of dough that is cooked with toppings. It is a comfort food held dear in many communities and is loved by young and old alike.

Here is our run down of the 'pizzas of the world'...

NEAPOLITAN *Birthplace:* Italy

The original, the first, the best. This is the dish that made Italian pizza world famous.

NEW YORK CITY PIZZA *Birthplace:* USA

With the very first Italians in America came pizza. NYC pizza is now probably the world's most famous pizza and is best served in large slices with garlic powder. (See page 232.)

CHICAGO DEEP DISH *Birthplace:* USA

NYC pizza's cousin and all the deeper to battle the freezing winters in Chicago. The crust is pushed into a deep pizza pan then stuffed with Wisconsin cheese, sausage, onion, bell pepper, tomatoes (along with whatever else you fancy), then slow-baked for 45 minutes until crunchy on top, juicy in the middle and crispy on the bottom. (See page 258.)

Deep dish, the ultimate cheese pull.

PISSALADIÈRE *Birthplace:* France

Way back when the region of Nice in France was part of the Italian kingdom, this 'Fritalian' dish originated. Bread dough is stretched into a shallow pie dish, then topped with slow-cooked tomatoes, caramelised onions and black olives. It is then criss-crossed with anchovy fillets and dusted with dried oregano, baked for 20 minutes and served (as always in France) with a good glass of white wine.

FLAMMKUCHEN *Birthplace:* Germany

Translated from German as 'flame cake' (sounds awesome BTW), this flatbread is a hit in the Alsace borders of France and Germany. It is traditionally rolled very thin and topped with crème fraîche, lardons, potatoes and onions before being baked in wood-fired ovens. The dish dates back to the 4th century, when farmers from Baden in Germany would bake bread once a week and use these thinly rolled-out flatbreads to test the heat of the oven.

LANGOS *Birthplace:* Hungary

This is a popular street food in Hungary, where the yeasted dough is made using mashed potato and flour which is then deep-fried to form a thick, crisp base. It is eaten with a sprinkle of salt or a topping of garlic butter, sour cream and grated cheese... woof.

MAN'OUSHE *Birthplace:* Levant Region

This is another dish we found on our travels in Lebanon. A yeasted flatbread, topped with a thick mix of za'atar spices, oil and sesame seeds, it is traditionally cooked on a domed cooking top over a wood fire (a little like a naan bread). They serve these up the mountains at ski resorts – the best post-piste snack ever.

KHACHAPURİ
Birthplace: Georgia

This is Georgia's national dish and is so popular that it is used as a way of measuring inflation. Calculated by the current cost of producing khachapuri, this method is literally called the 'Khachapuri Index'. (You really couldn't make this stuff up.) It is a leavened dough rolled out to a circle and topped with cheese. The sides are rolled inwards to create the shape of an eye, then the dish is topped with an egg and baked. Rip off the edges and dip in the molten cheese and egg. Dreamy.

Our tribute to the khachapuri. A collaboration with The Cheese Bar.

PASTRMAJLİJA *Birthplace:* Macedonia

Pastrmajlija is so popular in its home country of Macedonia that they have a festival in its honour every year. A yeasted bread dough is rolled out into an oval shape and topped with either cubed lamb or pork and sometimes egg.

ZAPİEKANKA *Birthplace:* Poland

A popular Polish street food since the 1970s, this is essentially a baguette halved lengthways and classically topped with sautéed mushrooms and cheese, then toasted until the cheese has melted. The name zapiekanka comes from the Polish verb *zapiekać*, meaning 'to bake a dish so that its ingredients combine, and a crispy, browned crust forms on top'. It is deemed great drunk food in Poland and is always served with Polish ketchup.

BULGOGİ PİZZA *Birthplace:* South Korea

This is the most popular pizza style in South Korea. Bulgogi is made with strips of beef that are heavily marinated in garlic, oyster sauce, sesame oil and soy. They are then barbecued at the table until they are sticky, tender and charred. To translate this into pizza form, the South Koreans spread the base with some of the marinade, then load it up with the beef and some onions, bell peppers, sweetcorn, mushrooms, mozzarella and black olives. This definitely isn't part of the 'less is more' group, but it is DELICIOUS!

FUGAZETTA *Birthplace:* Argentina

This is the Argentine variation of fugazza, which uses a dough pizza base method stuffed with fresh cheese then topped with sliced sweet onions before baking. When you cut into it, the cheese oozes out and makes for the best cheese pull you could ever hope for!

LAHMACUN *Birthplace:* Lebanon

This style of pizza is now popular all over the Levant. It calls for a mix of spiced ground meat with onions and bell peppers, which is then smeared on a flatbread and very quickly baked in a wood-fired oven. It is finished with a squeeze of lemon and sometimes a drizzle of pomegranate molasses. **Warning:** when we discovered these in Beirut, James ate ten for lunch…

I only had one chin when I went in!

Meeting the lemon bae of Beirut.

PİZZA PORTUGUESA *Birthplace:* Brazil

Pizza started getting popular in Brazil at the turn of the 20th century, when a huge influx of Italian immigrants arrived. Now, over 15% of people in Brazil are of Italian descent and Sao Paulo has the second-highest Italian population of any city in the world (more than Rome!). Pizza in Brazil is much like a carnival. Loud, big and not afraid of a bit of colour. One of the most famous pizzas is the Pizza Portuguesa, which features tomato sauce, Brazilian cheese, tomato slices, Calabrian sausage, ham, onions, bell peppers, boiled eggs and green or black olives. Not exactly a light bite. This big pizza is normally sliced and served on a plate. Eating more than one slice of this is deemed good going!

TLAYUDA *Birthplace:* Mexico

Coming in from the Mexican state of Oaxaca is an entry that even we think might be on the periphery of what you can call pizza. This is a corn tortilla that is fried or toasted on a grill, then topped with refried beans, lard, vegetables, meat, cabbage or lettuce, Oaxacan cheese and salsa. Delicious, thin and crispy, but perhaps not pizza.

PIZZA PILGRIMS CITY GUIDE

NAPLES

If you are going to visit one city on a pizza mission – this is the one.

This is it. The holy grail. The one that started it all (see our History of Pizza on page 24). If you love pizza, then Naples is an absolute must on your travel list. It is an amazing city with the most incredible energy (potentially derived from being built on the edge of an active volcano), and one thing is totally undeniable: they are proud of their pizza. Honestly, we have eaten so much pizza in Naples and have never *ever* had a bad one. Here are some places that should not be missed:

DA MICHELE

Da Michele is a lesson in focus and simplicity. They only have two pizzas on the menu – a Marinara with no cheese, or a classic Margherita. But don't let that put you off; the Margherita here is truly one of the most delicious things you can ever put in your mouth, with a light dough, fresh, acidic mozzarella and sweet tomato sauce. Just ask Julia Roberts – this is where she eats when she's not busy praying and loving! You'll have to queue but, believe us, it's worth it.

SORBILLO

Located on 'Pizza Street' – Via dei Tribunali – this is probably the most famous pizzeria in Naples. You will know it by the blue-and-white awning, and the hordes of people waiting outside for a table. But it is worth the wait (just grab a spritz from a nearby street trader) and is truly one of the best pizzas you can try in Naples. The dough is lighter than air and there is a huge selection of authentic toppings on offer. If you're lucky you will see Italy's number-one celebrity pizza chef, Gino Sorbillo himself, on site running the show, greeting the regulars and generally keeping his eye out to make sure the pizzas are as good as he expects!

Emanuele Liguor, first pizzaiolo, Da Michele.

Antonio Condurro, the last son of Michele, still working in the pizzeria.

Vincenzo Capuano.

Gino Sorbillo.

Dancing in the streets of Naples,
in lab coats, with Ciro Oliva –
accompanied by a plastic accordion.
Just a normal day!

DI MATTEO

Another great spot on Via dei Tribunali, Di Matteo is a no-nonsense pizzeria with two real specialties. One is the pizza (obvs) and the other is Naples' other gift to the culinary world, the *friggitoria*. They offer a huge selection of fried treats, from *fritattine di maccheroni* and potato crocchè to fried pizzas. The place is super-Neapolitan, with strip lighting and teams of waiters celebrating the latest Napoli goal in a back room. But it is the real deal, and a long-time favourite with the locals.

CONCETTINA AI TRE SANTE

For many years, the opinion of the pizzaioli (pizza makers) in Naples was that pizza was perfect – and if something is perfect, why change it? Pizzerias across the city were sticklers for the rules, and to do something off grid was a sacrilege. But Ciro Oliva, the newest pizza chef on the scene, has changed all that. His restaurant, Concettina ai Tre Sante, found off the beaten track in the Rione Sanità area of Naples, is pushing the boundaries of what pizza can be. And very successful it is too. This is the first pizzeria we have ever been to with a finishing section in the kitchen – to dress and top the pizzas as they come out the oven – and you won't believe what they manage to turn out in such a tiny space. Go for the tasting menu and see the heights and extremes that pizza really can reach.

SORBILLO FRIED PIZZA

Gino Sorbillo's influence stretches across Naples and he has a number of pizzerias dotted across the city offering a selection of different types of pizza. This hole-in-the-wall serves world-class fried pizza wrapped in paper for you to eat on the streets of Naples while checking out the Piazza del Plebiscito. Fried pizza is a must – and this is the place to try it.

50 KALO

It's a bit of a trek from the main action of the city, but Ciro Salvo's pizzeria is another great spot with queues around the block. The offerings are expansive and inventive – there are definitely one or two pizzas on the menu that you won't find anywhere else.

PIZZERIA BRANDI

This pizzeria at the bottom of the Via Umberto is the one where it all started. A lot of pizzerias in Naples claim to have invented the Margherita, but these guys have the letter on the wall from the Queen of Savoy to prove it. We buy it, and we're ever-thankful to Raffaele Esposito for his delicious creation. The pizza style here is old school but delicious, and the pizza oven is a thing of beauty. Eating here is a swankier experience than most (tablecloths everywhere) and the prices reflect that, but it is 100% worth a visit.

PIZZERIA VINCENZO CAPUANO

Vincenzo Capuano is a rising star in Naples, and it's clear that he's not interested in tradition. He is doing things his way – Maverick to the establishment's Ice Man. You can't knock him for it, and it is great to see another young gun moving with the times. He is a proponent of the 'canotto' style – huge, high, puffy crusts that dwarf the pizza and make it look like an inflatable dinghy (which is where the name comes from). And the excitement doesn't end there; with some really interesting creations and alternative classics on offer (not least the pizzas styled after the seven wonders of the world…), this is definitely worth the trip as a point of difference on your pizza journey. Follow with a nice walk down the Lungomare afterwards to work it all off!

PIZZERIA TRIANON

This is another very traditional Neapolitan place just a stone's throw from the Via dei Tribunali, serving really fantastic pizza in an established setting (and having done so for over 100 years). For whatever reason, this one seems to have slipped under the radar of the tourist guides, so a trip to Trianon will likely not involve fighting past hordes of visitors and a two-hour wait for a table. This is the insider's scoop, and a great place to get pizza, at a great price, especially if time is not on your side.

Via dei Tribunali, the centre of pizza in Naples/the world.

Lunchtime scenes at Da Michele.

Fried Pizza

FRİED PİZZA REALLY İS A THİNG.

Fried pizza is a big deal in Naples, with Gino Sorbillo, arguably the city's most famous pizza maker, having a shop entirely dedicated to it.

It was originally created after the war, when the going was incredibly tough for the people of Naples. Housewives were looking for a way to supplement their incomes, and traditional pizza ingredients such as mozzarella had become a luxury. This quickly led to people selling pizza fritta from their homes (as no pizza oven was required), stuffed with simple ingredients like ricotta and pork crackling. We actually visited one still existing home pizza fritta operation in the Quartieri Spagnoli area of Naples, our first ever taste of this delicious creation.

Today, pizza fritta comes in two forms. The first follows the 'calzone' method, made either by folding a disc of dough in half, or by sealing together two discs of dough placed on top of each other – this is then deep-fried in hot oil. It's stuffed with any combination of toppings, like provolone cheese, ricotta, Napoli salami and tomatoes. Although this sounds heavy, proper pizza fritta is lighter than air and a total triumph. It has so captured the spirit of the people of Naples that they have a saying: *fritto è buono tutto, anche l'aria* – 'everything tastes good fried, even the air'.

The second type of pizza fritta is called Montanara and is much simpler to make. A pizza dough base is fried so that it puffs up. It's then topped with tomato sauce and mozzarella, before spending a quick second in the pizza oven to finish it off.

PİZZA FRİTTA – FOLDED CALZONE STYLE

Serves: 4

Prep time: 20 minutes (assuming you have made the dough)

Cooking time: 5 minutes

Ingredients:

sunflower or other vegetable oil, for deep-frying

Neapolitan pizza dough (recipe on page 100)

handful of ricotta, for the filling

handful of Neapolitan black pepper salami, for the filling

Heat the oil in a large, heavy-based saucepan to 200°C/392°F. The oil should be deep enough to cover one pizza fritta at a time. Stretch the pizza dough into a flat circular base as per the method on page 101. Put the ricotta and salami in the centre. Fold the dough in half to enclose the fillings and pinch the edges closed. Holding the two ends, carefully and slowly lower it into the hot oil. Fry for about 30 seconds per side, until golden. Drain on kitchen paper. Eat while warm.

PİZZA CRUNCH

We must not forget that another city has a proud tradition of fried pizza – the city of Glasgow in Scotland. Pizza Crunch is simplicity itself: buy an already-cooked store-bought pizza, then take it to your local chippy who will batter and deep-fry it. And, we'll tell you for free, it is bloody delicious. There's never been a truer articulation of Mel Brooks' famous quote: **'Pizza is like sex, even when it is bad, it is good.'**

Sofia Loren –
the Grace Kelly of Naples.

Gino Sorbillo

Neapolitan Pizza's answer
to Cristiano Ronaldo.

Gino & Toto
Sorbillo
NYC 2017 · NAPOLI 1935 · MILANO 2014

Gino Sorbillo is surely the Cristiano Ronaldo
of Pizza (we hope you are impressed that we
walked straight past the chance for a 'crust' pun
there…). There's just something about Gino: his
perfect chef whites, his designer glasses, his
clean-shaven chin and shapely eyebrows…
he's just not made like the rest of us pizza chefs.
And just like Cristiano, Gino is incredibly (if
not a little annoyingly) talented. He is often the
man held responsible for globally elevating the
art of the pizza maker from a fast-food cook to
a highly skilled and revered role. He also is the
foremost champion for the traditional way of
making pizza in Naples, with all its simplicity

and celebration of local ingredients. So, what
else could this man have done to be crowned
the ultimate king of Naples pizza? Well, in
2012 he stood up to the infamous Naples mafia
Camorra by refusing to pay their 'pizzo', or
protection money, and, as a result, his pizzeria
was firebombed. But instead of running for the
hills, he cleaned up, turned the oven back on
and was serving pizza three days later… baller.

When you arrive at Sorbillo on Via dei
Tribunali you'll spot the huge blue-and-white
flag a mile off. Below, there is always a crowd
more fitting of a football stadium than a
pizzeria. Tourists and locals alike queue for

hours to get their opportunity for 30 minutes of pizza heaven. The pizza at his original pizzeria is characterised by being so massive that it hangs over the plate. The crust is quite small, which is a nod to the traditional way of doing things, potentially giving two fingers to the new wave of contemporary pizza with its canotto (Italian for 'rubber dinghy') crust. The dough Gino uses is very wet, resulting in a light crust that is also satisfyingly chewy (very hard to achieve!). The toppings are simple, locally sourced and AVPN (Associazione Verace Pizza Napoletana) approved. From the San Marzano tomatoes to the buffalo mozzarella and Caputo flour, everything about his pizza celebrates Naples. For us, this is one of the best places on the planet to try the truly original *pizza Napolitana* (forever overshadowed by the Margherita) – the Marinara. This pizza lets the tomato do the talking with no cheese at all but instead a

healthy slug of olive oil, a couple of cloves of garlic, basil and dried oregano. It's strange, but you don't miss the cheese; it tastes like the best pasta sauce ever, made right there on the dough.

Gino now has different pizza places popping up all over the city. His pizza fritta take-out joint serves up deep-fried calzones stuffed with all manner of deliciousness, from simple tomato and ricotta to cigoli and scarola leaves. His waterside place down on the Lungomare, called Lievito Madre al Mare, overlooks the bay of Naples and Mount Vesuvius, and serves up sourdough pizzas to the posh crowd of Naples.

Most recently, though, he's expanded outside of Naples into Milan, Rome, Genoa and New York. We're all for Sorbillo becoming a bit of a brand, as long as he keeps the pizza simple and doesn't mess with his current process. Why shouldn't there be a Sorbillo in every city? The world needs a Neapolitan pizza flag waver!

'PIZZA IS LIKE SEX. EVEN WHEN IT IS BAD,
IT IS GOOD.'

MEL BROOKS

PIZZA PILGRIMS CITY GUIDE

ROME

The Robin to Naples' Batman, Rome is no doubt a city that serves some fine pizza. While pizza in Rome is potentially less of a revered food than in its southern Italian counterpart, Rome is very happy to celebrate pizza in all its forms. Variety is the spice of life.

McCartney or Lennon, Man City or United, Oasis or Blur. These rivalries pale in comparison to who owns the Italian pizza crown between Naples and Rome. Sure, Naples has got the whole 'invention' thing, but Rome makes up for this with its versatility and maybe a certain sophistication that Naples lacks. Listen, we're not taking sides (not true) but on this page we promise to explain the pros of Roman pizza. Don't shoot the messenger and all that.

PIZZA AL TAGLIO

This style of pizza was invented in Rome but is popular across all of Italy. It directly translates as 'pizza by the cut' and is sold in long rectangular trays that sit on the counter for customers to point at. The pizza is cut using scissors into little rectangular slices and sold by weight. This style means that you don't have to choose one flavour but get a pic 'n' mix of what you like. The pizza has a thick but light crust, a lot like a focaccia, and the toppings are adventurous. At the moment, the king of this style of pizza in Rome is the man-mountain Gabriele Bonci. Back in 2011, when we met him, he was working out of a tiny shop near the Vatican called Pizzarium, which is now 'insta-famous'. The size of the shop was hilarious, he could hardly fit behind the counter and had the kind of firm, round belly that is only earned through hard work and dedication. He stormed into the kitchen, threw a handful of flour in his face and shouted that pizza is all about 'passion, sex and love! Must make loooooooove to the pizza!'. Then, in what can only be described as an awkward Italian pizza salsa, we squeezed round the kitchen, stretching the soft dough into the tray and blind baking the base before topping with hand-crushed tomatoes (done in a 'fe-fi-fo-fum' macho kind of way...), mozzarella, mortadella ham and artichokes, and baking. He took a huge bunch of sage and lit the end of it with a blowtorch. After taking a few 'tokes' and a short cackle, he smashed the flaming sage ball between his hands, scattering charred sage leaves all over the pizza. The pizza was incredible and, although he was some sort of pizza Goliath, he obviously had a great understanding of baking and flavour.

PİZZA ROMANA

After that intensely emasculating experience, we headed to Pizzeria Da Remo to try something altogether more delicate. Da Remo is an institution on the Roman pizza scene. The place is sparsely furnished with a massive green neon sign above the pizza oven. When you walk in, the waiters are always in a hurry and push you out of the way. With no bookings allowed, you mill around until someone decides they want to seat you. Trust us, it's well worth the wait. Start off with a big bottle of ice-cold Nastro Azzurro and some deep-fried zucchini flowers stuffed with mozzarella and anchovy. Then it's time for pizza. The pizza here is the definition of a classic wafer-thin crust. The classics include, of course, the Margherita, but also try the Diavola with spicy salami, and their sausage and mushroom creation, which definitely features in our Desert Island pizza list.

BAKERY PİZZA

There is a fantastic tradition in Rome of bakeries serving up great pizzas. The most famous spot for this is probably in the ancient square of Campo de' Fiori. This square has been famous for fire-cooked commodities for centuries, from coffee to pottery, but now is most well known for its baked goods. When you walk into Forno Campo de' Fiori bakery it's like going back 100 years. Wood panelling on the walls, stone floors and packed to the rafters with everything from huge loaves to cakes and biscuits. Even the pizza seems old fashioned here with the choice being between just two – rossa or bianca. Simple. Very light, the base is almost sourdough in texture and flavour. This is topped spartanly with tomato and olive oil, in case of the rossa, and literally just olive oil in the case of the bianca. To eat either feels like you're starring in the ultimate pizza purist play.

TRAPİZZİNO

The latest pizza invention in Rome happened in 2009, when Stefano Callegari was inspired by the classic 'crusts off' white bread sandwiches (called *tramezzini*), which can be found as a light snack in bars across Rome. He bakes six-inch-square bases, cuts them diagonally then opens up each triangle to create a pizza pocket ready to receive classic Roman pizza toppings like *pollo alla cacciatora* (hunter's chicken stew) and *polpette al sugo* (meatballs in tomato sauce).

So, what to say in summary? Roman pizza is wide-reaching and they have an answer for every occasion. The creative and adventurous styles make it an incredible city for a varied pizza crawl. But, we suppose the big question is, do any of these styles pip classic Neapolitan pizza to the pizza champion post? Absolutely not, don't make us laugh... 'Naples 'til we die, Naples 'til we die!' Sorry, we tried to stay impartial, but just couldn't.

Tomatoes

We use different varieties of tomatoes in the pizzerias: one for sauce and the other for keeping whole and using as a topping.

SAN MARZANO

The story goes that the tomato seed was given by the Viceroyalty of Peru to the King of Naples in 1770 as a gift. It was planted in the small town of San Marzano sul Sarno, just outside Naples (see our pizza pilgrimage on page 11). This town is nestled in the foothills of Vesuvius, where the soils are incredibly fertile. San Marzano tomatoes are considered by many to be the best sauce tomatoes in the world and, as such, are protected under Italian law or DOP. These tomatoes have thick flesh, few seeds and thin skins. The thin skins allow them to make the most of the Naples climate, soaking up the sun and in turn having a sweet and aromatic flavour.

The recipe we are asked most for in the pizzerias is our tomato sauce recipe. The truth is, it's the easiest recipe we have. We take great-quality canned tomatoes and mill them by hand through a wide sieve. We mill them this way for two reasons: firstly, it gives the sauce a great texture with actual pieces of tomato flesh (not completely broken down, like a passata); secondly, the seeds of a tomato are bitter, so if you blend them in a food processor that bitterness will go into the sauce – by hand milling we prevent the seeds from being blitzed and adding bitterness. The only ingredient we add to the tomatoes is salt. After that, it just gets a 60-second flash in the oven on the pizza. And there you have it – a sweet, salty, aromatic sauce that is fresh and full of flavour.

DATTERINI

We only use one other kind of tomato in the pizzerias: beautiful datterini tomatoes from Sicily. The word 'datterini' literally means 'little dates', and they're named as such on account of their intense sweetness, small size and elongated shape. They have thick skins, making them really robust, and few seeds, meaning more flesh! We use them as a topping on some of our pizzas. The other very noticeable characteristic of datterini tomatoes is their incredible aroma – add the stalks to sauces to impart a super floral flavour.

Fior di latte & Mozzarella

James was working for free at Di Matteo pizzeria in Naples just before we started Pizza Pilgrims. The mozzarella supplier arrived on his Vespa with the day's mozzarella. He put down his espresso, signalled for James to come over and said,

'You the English guy?'

'Yup...'

'Taste this mozzarella!'

It was unlike any mozzarella we'd tried before. You could taste the fresh milk and acidity, and the texture was tougher than we are used to in the UK, with more elasticity and bite.

'You will never get mozz like this in London.'

And he was right. The mozzarella you get in Naples, and which is made and eaten on the same day, is something worth travelling for. We work really hard to get our mozzarella to our pizzerias as quickly as is humanly possible but, the truth is, it still takes days. There's something quite comforting to know that however hard we try to make the best pizza, it will never be quite as good as in Naples. We're OK with that; they did invent it.

It is worth noting, that when it comes to discussing Mozzarella in the context of Neapolitan Pizza, you could be talking about two different products. The first is 'fior di latte', which is the mozzarella used as standard on a Neapolitan Margherita and which is made with cow's milk (the name translated means 'flower of milk'). Mozzarella made with buffalo milk is referred to as 'bufala' (or 'Mozzarella di Bufala Campana' to give it the full name). This distinction is a really important one as bufala is a much creamier, wetter product than fior di latte. Make sure you ask specifically for bufala in Naples if that is what you would like on your pizza.

MAKİNG YOUR OWN FİOR Dİ LATTE MOZZARELLA

On the face of it, this could be seen as a really simple way to make cheese. And in many ways, it is. We've tried this a few times at home and you can create something that could only be described as mozzarella. However, as with so many Italian crafts, it takes a lifetime to master. So, who better to hand you over to for this process than our good friend, and owner of Latteria Sorrentina in Naples, Giovanni. This is how they make mozzarella the right way...

'The key to great mozzarella is twofold: the milk and the experience...'

1. We heat full-fat Italian milk (from grass-fed cows) gently with the microbiological rennet (ethical and suitable for vegetarians) until it's approximately 30–32°C/86–89°F. This lets the caseins separate from the wheys. The exact point of maturation for the curds is an art that comes with practice, and will in turn deliver the best cheese.

2. Once the curds have set, the heat is turned off and the cheese is cut.

3. The curds are left to cool in the whey and then are drained.

4. At this point, we begin the traditional process of 'spinning'. The curds are stirred together with some of the whey and heated to above 82°C/179°F. Traditionally, spinning is done in a wooden bowl with a long wooden spoon. The curds are placed in the bowl and then the whey is poured over the top. Using the spoon, you pull the curds into long stretches. Usually after 3–4 pulls the cheese will take on a shine and smoothness. The curds are then balled.

5. The balls are rested for at least 15 minutes in room-temperature salted water. This imparts a good saltiness to the mozzarella. It is important not to rest it in ice-cold water as you will end up with a tough and rubbery mozzarella.

6. Once rested, store in salted water until needed.

Note: Supermarket milk is pasteurised at temperatures of up to 138°C/276°F, which means that it cannot be made into mozzarella.

Left: Thom & James with The Mozzarella Kings, Giovanni Amodio and Franco Amodio.

Parmesan

One of Italy's hero products – which has secretly been living on your pizza all this time!

Parmesan is 100% identified with Italy and remains one the products that they are most proud of (and most reluctant to let leave their shores; the Italians are the masters of keeping the good stuff for themselves). Parmesan is so revered in Italy that you can use wheels of it as collateral against a bank loan!

Parmigiano-Reggiano (the name is derived from the two towns near to the home of its production, Parma and Reggio Emilia) is, on the face of it, a very simple product. It only contains three ingredients: milk, salt and rennet. But through the mysterious combination of expertise and, more importantly, time, it morphs into a product with incredible complexity, balance and flavour that you just wouldn't believe. It really is one of those products that, when you see it being made, makes you wonder how anyone discovered how great it would turn out in the end.

Milk is delivered to the factory twice a day, where the master cheese maker oversees its blending and cooking in preparation for the production of every individual Parmesan wheel. He is only paid for the ones that end up passing stringent tests after months of curing, so it's in his best interests to stay focused.

In order to be considered actual Parmesan, the cheese needs to cure for at least 12 months; however, the best Parmesan (with the fullest flavour and little protein deposits that make for a satisfying crunchiness) is cured for at least 36 months.

Every Parmesan supplier will always have a secret stash of cheese that has been aged even longer than this – that no one will ever get their hands on!

We visited a Parmesan production facility on our original pilgrimage and, let's just say, they took it pretty seriously. The maturing rooms contained about 25,000 wheels of Parmesan at various stages of maturation, at a total value of around ten million euros! So, we guess it's fair enough that they take it seriously.

We know what you are thinking: why is this relevant to pizza? Get to the point! Well, certainly in the case of traditional Neapolitan rules, Parmesan is added to almost every single pizza. It adds a great umami hit and complements the flavours on Neapolitan Margherita perfectly.

Divisive Ingredients

Ever since there have been people, there have been arguments as to what should, and what should not, go on their pizza. The arguments that are sparked over a pizza menu have ended friendships and marriages. We think it's fair to say these are some of the moments when people understand each other the least. Below is a list of some of the most divisive ingredients we've come across.

PİNEAPPLE

Pineapple on pizza was first created by a six-foot, long-haired Hawaiian surfer called Uluwehi... NAAAAAT! Despite its truly tropical name, the Hawaiian pizza was invented in the sixties by a retired Greek cook called Sam Panopoulos at the Satellite Restaurant in Chatham, Ontario. He said he just had some pineapple in stock so tried it on the pizza and, right from the get go, it divided opinion. He said: 'Some people loved it and others said "are you crazy?!"'. It's taken us a long time to come to terms with it, but, we can now proudly say that we love pineapple on pizza – and we will fight you over it! Even the god of pizza, Franco Pepe (see page 80), has a pizza with pineapple on it!

PASTA

In Naples they really love two things: pizza and pasta. However, they very much take the 'too much of a good thing' mentality seriously and so the idea of pasta on pizza is sacrilegious. We learned this the hard way when we created a guest pizza for our menu featuring our other favourite dish, pasta carbonara (see page 122). We topped a white pizza with olive oil, roasted pancetta, mozzarella, Parmesan, strands of bucatini pasta and egg yolk. There's no other way to describe it than jaw-droppingly DELICIOUS! On the day we launched it we got a number of calls and emails from our Neapolitan chefs asking for a 'serious chat' and in one case a threat of resignation. It took over a week to convince everyone that this was just for fun, and not a permanent feature on the menu. Thankfully no chefs left, and it ended up being one of our best-selling pizzas. Go figure!

Andrea Di Maio –
Pizza Pilgrims pizzaiolo.

ANCHOVIES

Now, even the Italians break their own rule here. You often hear in Italy, 'fish and cheese should never be eaten together!', but they flagrantly disregard this rule with anchovies. To understand why, you have to go back to the beginning (of pizza…). Pizza came into existence as a peasant food, and one of the toppings most abundantly available to the poor of southern Italy were anchovies. The Mediterranean was full of them and they could be preserved very easily in a little salt or oil. So, anchovies were first put on pizza for survival reasons, for essential protein. Since then, anchovies have remained synonymous with pizza but one that seems to put you in the 'weird food eater' category. The Olsen twins sing of their hate of anchovies on pizza in their infamous 'pizza rap', but they clearly cannot be trusted. On the other hand, Fry from *Futurama* spends a whole episode championing the little fish on pizza!

CHICKEN

Now, this one is a thinker. Every Italian worth their *sale* will run a mile at the idea of chicken on pizza. We've had this argument with our pizza chefs and they will shout until they are blue in the face, but can't actually give a reason as to why they're against it. We've trawled the internet and can't find any strong evidence to cling to. Perhaps the texture of chicken is too close to the dough? Maybe they are both performing the same job, acting as vehicles for flavour? Outside of Italy chicken on pizza seems to be loved the world over, with BBQ chicken being voted in the top three ingredients by Domino's customers in the US. We think this is just one of the rules we'll have to put in the same category as 'no cappuccinos after midday' – those that seem to happen for no reason but that Italians live and die by.

CURRY BANANA

This one is just plain bizarre, coming from glorious Sweden, the country that brought you *surströmming*, a putrefied canned fish that is so smelly it is illegal to open indoors. We tried the stuff once and it was the only time in our lives that we were able to *see* a smell! So, maybe it's not so surprising that one of the most popular pizzas in Sweden is a Margherita topped with sliced banana, curry powder and peanuts. We took the time to make this with our chefs, hoping it would be like a twist on a Hawaiian… it was not. It tasted like a smoothie on a pizza but with added curry. We dare you, next time you're making pizza at home, grab a banana and some curry powder and… completely ruin it!

Making Pizza at Home

We are living in unprecedented times people! It wasn't too long ago that your best bet for making pizza at home was either dropping £5k on a full-blown, brick pizza oven or popping the box on a frozen pizza and waiting 16 minutes for a paradoxically crispy and doughy, tomato-ketchup mess that would burn the roof of your mouth. How glorious it is to live in a modern age where home pizza perfection is so easily available!

ROCCBOX

If Steve Jobs designed a pizza oven, this would be it. The Roccbox reminds us of the early iMacs for their sleek design. For us, this oven replicates the conditions of our Neapolitan pizza ovens the best. The gas fire gives a great char and the stone floor allows the crust to rise beautifully. An even bigger seal of approval is that we've noticed a lot of street food traders and restaurants using these in their kitchens – confirmation that it's a hard worker!

COB OVEN

So, just a heads up, you are going to need some space for this one! It's hard to say whether this is more art project than operation-pizza-oven but it's fun to do and you feel like a hero once it's done. This is how we did it: First thing you need is some clay-rich soil (we Googled where in London has clay soil and then drove around until we found some roadworks – after asking nicely, they let us shovel an Ikea bag's worth of soil into the car). Next, you need to get some sand and straw, which we easily got from the local hardware store. Lay out a tarpaulin in the garden and then mix together about two-parts clay soil, one-part sand and one-part straw. You then add as much water as you need to make a thick clay cement. Much like crushing grapes, you can use your feet to squelch the clay together until you have a nice smooth and consistent cement. Next, take some fire bricks (which you can order online) and arrange them in a circle on a flat (preferably concrete) outdoor surface. Then mix some more sand with a little water so it sticks together and start piling it up to create a tall and round mound in the centre of your bricks, leaving about 10cm/4in around the internal edge. Cover the sand with pages of wet newspaper to create a solid(ish) dome shape. Take your clay cement and begin to cover the sand mound entirely. You should aim for a 10cm/4in

James' first oven, made out of a bin, some mud and a tennis ball tube.

depth all the way around. Once totally covered, cut a mouth in your oven where you want the front to be, big enough to slide a pizza through. The mouth should be two-thirds of the height of the internal dome height to allow for good air flow. Allow to dry for a couple of hours then use your hand to dig out all of the sand and – ta-da! – you have a pizza oven. Leave it another few hours to dry a little more, then light a small fire in the oven. This will fire the clay and solidify the oven. Add wood to the fire slowly until you have a larger fire and then leave to burn out overnight. The next day you are ready to make pizza! Easy!

PIZZA STONE

Hmmm… the pizza stone. As heavy as it is *terrible* at making great pizza. At about £30 a pop we can see why so many people bought them. But, here's the problem: they get too hot for shop-bought pizzas and not hot enough for homemade pizzas. When you drop a homemade pizza with raw dough onto a pizza stone the temperature immediately drops and a 200°C/400°F/Gas 6 oven just doesn't have enough fire power to give the pizza the nice crisp bottom it deserves and to allow the crust to rise properly. Our advice is, if you want to cook pizza this way, then just go to your local building shop and buy a stone slab for two quid. Dodge the branded kit – it's a rip-off!

FRYING PAN PIZZA

OK, bias warning… this is our method! We came up with this technique in the first week we started Pizza Pilgrims. We'd just got our van with the pizza oven back from the oven manufacturer and invited 50 friends round as a test run. In our naivety, we lit the oven way too late and the pizzas were coming out looking anaemic. So, we got a pan screaming hot on the hob, dropped the pizza in the pan and instantly the crust rose and the bottom browned beautifully. We finished the pizza under a hot grill (broiler) and the party was saved. We know we're biased, but we think this method wins hands down. It creates a beautiful, light and fluffy pizza and all you need is a frying pan, which costs about £15. Pizza to the people! See our full method on page 102.

Check out that CRUST!

Pulling this expression is optional.

'THERE IS NO ASPECT, NO FACET, NO MOMENT OF LIFE THAT CAN'T BE IMPROVED WITH PIZZA.'

DARIA

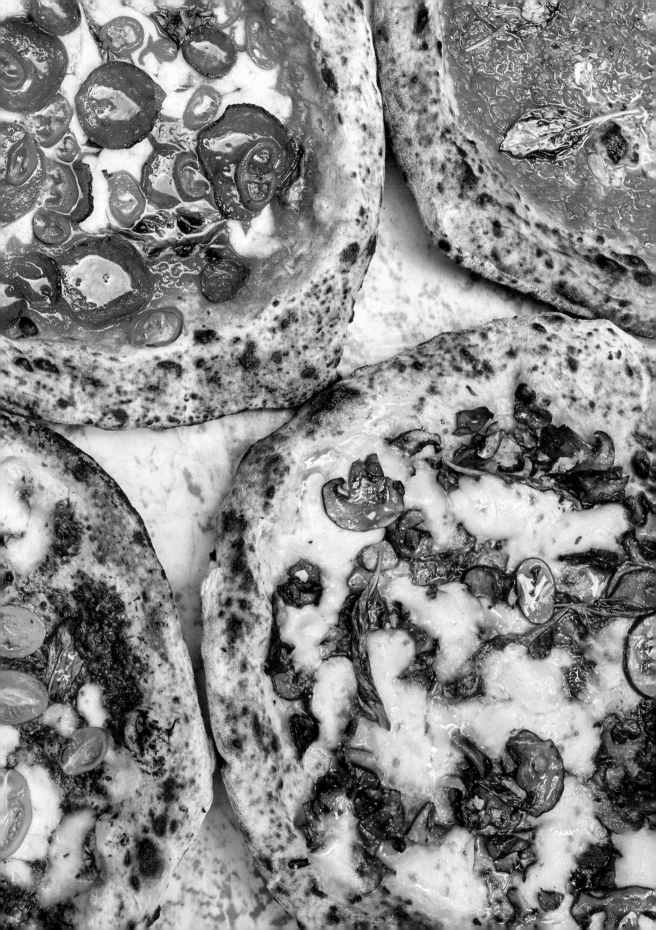

Franco Pepe

The best pizzaiolo in the world.

We know that it seems a bit strange that the best pizzaiolo in the world is not based in Naples, but Franco Pepe's restaurant Pepe in Grani really takes pizza to the next level. If anywhere was going to get a Michelin star for making pizza, this would be the place.

Now, stating that Franco Pepe is 'the best pizzaiolo in the world' is wildly contentious (and essentially an impossibility – one man's Dominos is another man's sourdough and all that) but, while writing this book, we had to make the pilgrimage out to Franco's restaurant, in the small town of Caiazzo in Italy, to see what all the fuss is about. And, let us tell you, Franco sure knows his way around a pizza…

Pepe
I N G R A N I
• • •

Thom+James: Hey Franco, why did you name your pizzeria Pepe in Grani?

Franco: My father already runs a restaurant called Pizzeria Pepe, so I had to come up with something different! The word *pepe* in Italian means 'pepper' and *grani* means 'grains' or 'corns'. So, it's a play on words with my family name and 'peppercorns'.

Thom+James: Why do you think people love pizza so much?

Franco: Pizza has spread all around the world because it is simple and easy to understand. It's a food for people to connect over.

Thom+James: What do you want to achieve with your pizza?

Franco: I'm interested in the science and nutrition of it all. When people eat my pizza, I want it to include everything needed for a balanced meal. Traditionally, pizza hasn't been seen as the healthiest of foods – I want to change this. I consult with a nutritionist to ensure each of my pizzas includes a healthy balance of ingredients. For example, I've added anchovies to my Marinara to up the protein content of the pizza. It's not necessarily traditional, but it's *balanced*. Health and pizza are both really important to me, and at Pepe in Grani I'm able to combine the two.

Thom+James: And is your pizza still evolving? Are you still learning?

Franco: The learning never stops! I was taught this by my father and it's something I've always carried with me. I'm always looking to make better pizza and always discovering new things about it. Up until recently, everything I've done has been about mastering authentic Neapolitan pizza. Now, I'm looking beyond just 'authentic' to the future of pizza. I went on holiday to Iscia recently and visited a freshwater spring there. I found out that the water in the spring is full of nutrients. Using this water to make my pizza dough means I can use 40% less salt and yeast, which is incredible!

Thom+James: If you don't mind us asking, what's your favourite pizza?

Franco: Easy question. The calzone with scarola that my father used to make for me.

Thom+James: Thanks Franco, it's been an honour to eat at Pepe in Grani and have the opportunity to chat with you.

Pepe in Grani è un luogo dove fermarsi e ragionare su un antico cibo popolare, dove un disco di pasta racconta i sapori dell'Alto Casertano e la passione di un moderno artigiano.
Da noi non troverete ritmi frenetici: lavoriamo nel rispetto di gesti antichi per una pizza dai sapori d'altri tempi.

Pepe
IN GRANI

Pizza-Loving Celebrities

JENNIFER LAWRENCE

Probably one of the greatest pizza-loving celebrities out there, Jennifer Lawrence certainly knows about pizza, and is not afraid to tell the world about it. Believe it or not, her favourite pizza looks more like a sandwich – a distinctive sandwich, to say the least. Her beloved creation comprises southern chilli and noodles sandwiched between two slices of pizza, which she claims is her best invention to date.

AMY SCHUMER

Another celebrity who loves her pizza spicy is Amy Schumer. Her regular pizza order includes toppings like pepperoni and jalapeños. However, don't forget to add a side of ranch sauce, or she is not eating that pizza. She even devoted an entire comedy sketch in honour of the subject.

CHANCE THE RAPPER

While he cannot stay away from a traditional Chicago-style deep-dish pizza, Chance the Rapper stays classic with pepperoni because, 'why mess up something so pure?' he explained while discussing pizza at the VMAs.

KENDALL JENNER & KHLOE KARDASHIAN

These Kardashian sisters are pizza purists. They stick to the basics, no matter what. Both Kendall and Khloe have shown their devotion to Margherita on their social media accounts and countless *Keeping Up with the Kardashians* episodes.

BEYONCÉ

Although Beyoncé is known for favouring vegan pizzas, her to-go pizza choice involves extra tomato sauce and jalapeños. In fact, the famous singer confessed to *Beat* magazine that she keeps a bottle of spicy sauce in her bag – because you never know when you need that extra hit of spice.

ED SHEERAN

The famous English songwriter has a unique idea about a pizza and its toppings, which he explained in a lengthy tweet. For Sheeran, his perfect pizza begins with a traditional sauce and cheese pie. He then he tops the pizza with fries, rolls the whole thing up, and then dips it in ketchup before he indulges in this tasty creation.

KATE MIDDLETON

Royals are no strangers to the divinity of pizza. Kate Middleton is said to be an avid pizza lover, and while on many trips to the US, she often indulges in a royal pizza featuring prosciutto and sausage toppings.

MILEY CYRUS

The actress and singer is another celebrity with a crush on pizza. Cyrus always shows her love for pizza by posting photos of her pizza pillows, pizza onesies, pizza jackets, etc. In fact, the singer even had a pizza-themed party for her 22nd birthday! For Miley, the cheesier the better, no need to add anything else.

LEBRON JAMES

The NBA player knows his pizza and keeps up with his high-protein diet. LeBron uses a pizza dough transporter for his many protein preferences. The craziest and biggest pizza order we've seen is probably his favourite: high-rise pizza dough with spicy sauce, extra mozzarella, Parmesan, grilled chicken, turkey meatballs, banana peppers, green bell peppers, red onions, fresh basil, garlic, spinach, sea salt, oregano, rocket (arugula), Kalamata olives and olive oil. It has 16 toppings! You can see the actual creation on his Instagram.

CHRISSY TEIGEN

Chrissy takes pizza-loving to the extreme – by having pizza for breakfast. Apparently it got her through pregnancy, though, so we're not here to judge (we're actually massive fans of breakfast pizza – see our Dishoom collab on page 192).

GEORGE CLINTON, PARLIAMENT FUNKADELIC

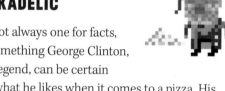

He's not always one for facts, but something George Clinton, funk legend, can be certain of, is what he likes when it comes to a pizza. His preference? A thin crust. 'It's all in how you toss the pizza,' he says, not incorrectly. And his pizza location of choice? Naples? New Haven? Nope – North Newark. You heard it here first…

DEC DONNELLY

One thing we can be sure of is what Dec does not like on his pizza – pineapple. In 2018 he announced on *I'm a Celebrity Get Me Out of Here* that 'only perverts put pineapple on pizza'. Very clear. He joins a large group on this one, including Gordon Ramsay and the Prime Minister of Iceland (who almost tried to ban it). That said, Dwayne 'The Rock' Johnson is a fan of pineapple on pizza, so that might just be the end of the debate…

SCARLETT JOHANSSON

'I love pizza with anything except pineapple or anchovies on the top.'

Antimo Caputo

The Pablo Escobar of the pizza world
(in a nice way…)

We first met Antimo Caputo, owner of the famous Caputo Flour Mill in the centre of Naples, on our original pilgrimage in 2011. At the time, we knew nothing about pizza, didn't speak a word of Italian (still don't!) and must have seemed pretty mad turning up in our three-wheeled Ape. But Antimo really took the time to explain what Caputo was about, what sets it apart and why it remains the best pizza flour in all of Italy. We have been friends ever since and, having visited the mill almost twenty times now, his undying passion for his product, as well as his constant desire to improve and innovate, is evident (check out their new 'Nuvola flour' for extra puffy canotto-style crusts).

CAPUTO
1924
Il mulino di Napoli

We sat down with Antimo on our latest trip to Naples to get a little insight into the company, the global pizza scene and the next steps for the world of flour!

Thom+James: What makes a great pizza?

Antimo: In my opinion, pizza has a soul. And the soul of pizza is the pizza makers in Napoli. It's something to share, something popular, something to make you happy. To me, pizza is not something to be taken too seriously – without the fun, it is not the pizza that Naples loves.

Thom+James: Can you put your finger on why people love pizza so much?

Antimo: Because, number one, it is very easy. It is easy to understand. It is also easy to share, and it's simple in its essence. People love all these things. Today, we are what we eat. I eat because I want an experience; that could be a three-Michelin-star experience on the one hand, or it could be pizza on the other – something you can eat anywhere in the world. When I go to New York, I go to all the pizzerias to understand what is happening in the world of pizza. You just can't have an issue with how pizza is evolving. The pizza of today is very different in Naples to how it was 50 years ago, and the pizza you eat in New York today is not the one started in Lombardi's – it's completely different. Pizza can evolve with people due to its inherent simplicity.

Thom+James: Can you explain the story behind your flour?

Antimo: Our Nuvola flour is very simple. It was born for a new generation of pizza makers. They work with the clock – they schedule everything, even their dough – and the whole process is planned out, so the flour has to match this. Nuvola is like a Ferrari, a race car. When you drive a race car you have to battle it and you have to drive very carefully and, if you do so, you will get an amazing performance. But if you get it wrong – BANG – you will crash. You have to know how to control Nuvola: how to use salt, which yeast to use, the oven temperature, the hydration, the timing. If you grasp this you can achieve a fantastic, light, crispy, hollow crust with a strong taste. Our Caputo Blue flour, on the other hand, is like a Mercedes – it is a great product but more forgiving. Our Caputo Gluten-Free is doing well and we have a separate company in Bergamo to produce this for us. There are a lot of good gluten-free flours out there, but we have studied it hard and have come up with something that really matches the traditional flavour, in our opinion.

Thom+James: Do you think that Italy still makes the best pizza?

Antimo: To be honest, in Naples you can eat the most historical pizza in the world, but to say it is the best is impossible. The world of pizza is now so huge that you can never say which is the definitive best pizza. My idea is that there are global capitals of pizza around the world – one is Napoli, one is New York, one is Sao Paulo – and they all make wonderful pizza. Even London and Paris today are doing exciting things – these are the next ones to watch for me. Of course, our access to ingredients in Italy is fantastic. In my mind, Neapolitan pizza paved the way to the idea of an artisanal pizza. It is where it started and it was the first to get STG (*Specialità Tradizionale Garantita*) certification to protect its production method. It has a great story. It is also now protected by UNESCO – so *Pizza Napoletena* is a concept that is 100% artisanal. We simply opened the door to the rest of the world.

Thom+James: Caputo is obviously a flour company. So, if the world stopped eating pizza tomorrow, what percentage of your flour sold is not used to make pizza?

Antimo: 80% of the flour we currently sell is used to make pizza. People also use it for fresh pasta, cakes, bread – but most of it is pizza.

Thom+James: Where are the newest pizza markets? Which countries surprised you when they first ordered flour from you?

Antimo: New Zealand! And Hawaii!

Thom+James: So, I guess this brings us naturally to the most important question... What do you think about pineapple on pizza?

Antimo: No!

Thom+James: Strawberries?

Antimo: Hmm, maybe. At least they're not as sweet as pineapple! And they look good – you eat with your eyes, after all.

Thom+James: So, every country will one day be using Caputo flour?

Antimo: We hope so!

Team Pizza Pilgrims at the Caputo flour mill in Naples.

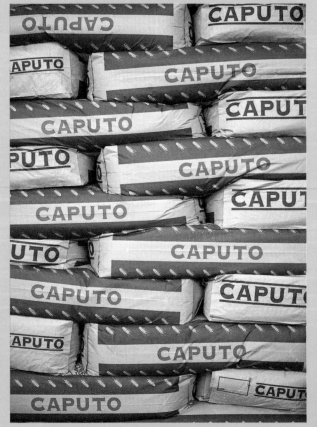

Mauro Caputo.

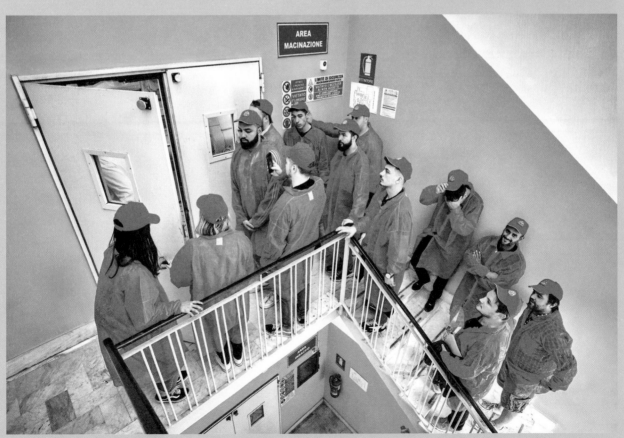

PIZZA DOUGH IS ALIVE

By Pizza Pilgrims' First Chef Tom Mullin

There is nothing more debated within pizza than dough. It's the first thing pizza fanatics like us will look at. It's what we constantly think about and what we reminisce about. If I think back to the best slice of pizza I've ever had, sure I remember the sweet tomato and the creamy mozzarella, but what I can really recall is the dough and its pillows of crust seasoned with those toppings. The crust, which has been charred with attitude, giving just a slight chewiness, melting in your mouth, leaves you eager for another slice. That's Neapolitan pizza.

Usually made with very few ingredients but with a fierce amount of accuracy, it's a complex simplicity. One of the coolest things I've learned while obsessing over pizza is that as chefs (*pizzaiolo* in Italian) we are literally creating and capturing life in the form of dough – introducing water to flour, with the help of living yeast cells, we mould and nurture. Our dough is a living and very much breathing thing.

Neapolitan pizza dough relies on only the basic bread ingredients of flour, water, salt and yeast, but like we've found in many southern Italian recipes, what makes the difference is how the ingredients are used. A simple recipe becomes so much more when you take a closer look at how precisely the ingredients are balanced by a pizzaiolo.

With that balance there is one more very significant ingredient which often gets overlooked, and that is time. Time is probably the greatest and most important ingredient in making dough. In some way, similar to us, dough needs time to mature and develop.

FLOUR

Flour is the most abundant ingredient in our dough and really sets the tone for the rest of the pizza, so we'll need to give it plenty of attention. Our goal is to make a soft and long-rising dough. There will be many variables in achieving this, but when it comes to flour the two main attributes are the grain fineness and the strength.

Grain Fineness

In pizza and pasta dough recipes we often see this term double zero or '00'. It has good reason to be so beloved in the pizza world, but first we need to understand what makes flour 'double zero'.

Italy has a numerical system for grading flours which is 2, 1, 0 and 00, and these indicate how fine the flour is milled. Grade 2 is the coarser end of the scale, which is comparable to wholewheat or brown flour. As we go down the numbers, the flour is milled more and more until 00, which is ground to an extreme fineness. So fine it's almost like a dust. It's this 00 flour which gives a silky-smooth feel to the classic Neapolitan pizza dough.

Strength

Protein equals strength, and to explain what that means we're going to get a little bit scientific. When mixed with water, protein molecules in the flour bind together to produce strands of gluten. The network of gluten strands form strong elastic bonds within the dough. The tighter the elastic bonds, the stronger the dough. The amount of protein can vary across all grades of flour, depending on the type of wheat and its growing conditions.

Protein is measured as a percentage of the flour weight. This information is available on most packaging, displayed as protein grams per 100 grams of flour, so, simply, 12g equals 12% protein. As a quick reference, flour with 13% or more protein is referred to as strong or hard flour, 11% or less referred to as soft or weak flour. A loaf of bread is usually made with strong flour to give it real body and chew, while cakes and pastry are usually made with a softer flour for a more delicate, short texture.

So for the soft and long-rising dough we opt for the very fine 00 flour with a protein content of 12.5%. Just slightly above the medium strength. This is just strong enough to hold all the air as the dough slowly rises, but soft enough to create a light crust. This balanced flour has got our dough off to a great start.

The Original Flour

When pizza first emerged in Naples they probably used something similar to wholewheat flour, but when refined white flour became all the rage at the turn of the 19th century they also started using the finer milled flour to make silky-smooth pizza dough. 00 flour still stands as the traditional choice today in most pizzerias in Naples and around the world, but some are experimenting and evolving the dough with different types and combinations of flours.

Mulino Caputo

At Pizza Pilgrims we specifically use Caputo Blue Pizzeria Flour. We have made the pilgrimage many times to the Caputo mill (see page 94), to see their flour being made and to marvel at how much intricacy and research goes into sourcing and producing what is some of the best flour in the world. They achieve their own balance, which is a constant activity of adjusting mixes of grains and reacting to fluctuating weather patterns and growth conditions from around the world.

ITALY	UK
2	Wholewheat
1	Plain/All-Purpose
0	Bread Flour
00	Cake Flour

Fig i. **Italian to UK/US flour**

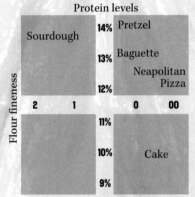

Fig ii. **Typical flour milling and protein levels for baked goods**

WATER

Water, while a seemingly simple ingredient, plays a vital role as the solvent in which the other ingredients are combined and dispersed evenly throughout the dough. It also greatly influences the texture. Not enough water makes the dough stiff and tight. Too much water makes it wet and sticky. To get it just right we use a volume of water equivalent to 62% of the flour weight. In baking terms it's called the dough hydration, and you can apply this percentage to whatever amount of flour you are using to determine the correct amount of water. So for 1000g of flour, we calculate that we would need 620ml water.

Baker Percentages

This is a common method used in baking to calculate the amounts of ingredients. As flour is regarded as the heaviest ingredient, all other ingredients are expressed as a percentage of that total flour weight. This allows recipes to be quickly scaled up and down, or to make accurate adjustments to ingredients. To calculate, we simply divide the weight of the ingredient by the total weight of the flour and multiply by 100:

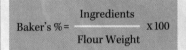

$$\text{Baker's \%} = \frac{\text{Ingredients}}{\text{Flour Weight}} \times 100$$

Fig iii. **Baker Percentages**

SALT

Salt makes pizza dough taste good. If you imagine flavour is a sound, adding salt would be like turning the volume up loud. In addition, it quietly works on some chemistry in the background by using its preservative qualities to control the rate of fermentation. By slowing things down it gives our dough more time to mature and develop flavour.

Typical bread dough uses about 2% salt (remember our baker percentages), but for Neapolitan pizza we turn the volume up a bit louder and go for 3% salt. Neapolitan pizza is quite thin, so we need maximum taste in the small layer of crust.

Use a good-quality fine sea salt. Try to avoid any table salt or iodised salt as they tend to be processed and not beneficial for flavour.

A Pizzaiolo Never Forgets

You would think it's a fool-proof recipe having very few ingredients; however, they are all absolutely crucial to the dough – without one the dough simply won't work. I learnt this the hard way on my second weekend of our first pizzeria on Dean Street, Soho. That evening something wasn't right. The pizzas were coming out flat, a bit beige and bland, and the customers noticed. The chefs and I checked everything; maybe the dough was too cold? Maybe the oven wasn't hot enough? But when I investigated the dough room in the basement, I found 750g of salt, perfectly measured out, but not in the dough... To this day, I still taste a piece of raw dough after mixing to ensure I remembered the salt.

YEAST

Probably the most fascinating ingredient, yeast is the living element in dough. It's a micro-organism with a sweet tooth. Yeast consumes the sugars from the flour and 'burps' out carbon dioxide. It's this carbon dioxide which swells the gluten network, filling the dough with tiny air bubbles and making it rise.

As the dough expands, yeast also takes part in fermentation. In a very similar process to how beer or wine is made, this fermentation breaks down starches into acids and alcohol, developing all the lovely flavours you get from bread. Time is crucial for this fermentation. Controlling the rate of fermentation is mainly achieved by varying the amount of yeast used as well as the temperature of the dough.

We want to use a very low amount of yeast, to make it work long and hard on fermenting. In the pizzeria we use on average an amount of yeast equivalent to 0.05% of the flour weight. That is 0.5g of yeast for every 1000g of flour. But it doesn't stop there, as yeast is very sensitive to temperature, speeding up in warmer environments and slowing down when it's colder. To counter, we use more yeast when it's colder, and less when it's warmer.

In the summer we may drop the yeast as low as 0.02% and in the winter we may bump it up to near 0.1%.

At home, you're likely using a kilo or two of flour, so measuring anything less than 1g of yeast is going to be pretty difficult. As a standard we recommend using 0.2% yeast which equates to 2g of yeast for every 1000g of flour.

The particular species of yeast for bread baking can be commercially manufactured and is available in 3 forms:

Fresh Yeast

Also known as compressed or cake yeast, is our preferred format here. It's naturally active, easily measured and offers more control on our fermentation rate, making it perfect for a slow rise. It can often be purchased from bakeries or some pizzerias, and is also available in larger supermarkets that have dedicated in-store bakeries – just ask. You can also order online.

Active Dry Yeast

This is a good second choice. It is essentially the same but with moisture removed and ground up into granules. To adjust a recipe to active dry yeast multiply the fresh quantity by 0.4.

Instant Yeast

Also known as fast acting yeast, this is formulated for rapid rising – not exactly suitable for our long fermentation, so avoid if possible. Still, if needs must, to adjust the recipe for instant yeast multiply the fresh quantity by 0.33.

KNEADING & MIXING

We mix our dough based on the below percentages:

'00' Flour (100%)
Water (62%)
Fine Sea Salt (3%)
Fresh Yeast (0.2%)

In the pizzerias, we have machines to mix our dough, but at home you may be relying on your hands to work the magic. Some may prefer to mix the ingredients in a bowl or dough hook mixer, both of which are great, but we're going to end up kneading by hand on the table top anyway so I prefer to avoid washing up more utensils than needed and just do everything with my hands, traditional style, pretending I'm as authentic or as good as my Neapolitan mates.

Chefy tip: have all your ingredients measured out before you begin. Measuring each ingredient as you need it isn't fun, and you'll look like a pro as you whip through the recipe with grace.

First the yeast is dissolved in the water. This will help it disperse evenly throughout the dough and ensure it gets maximum exposure to all the starch in the flour. It's crucially important we use tepid water. Remember, yeast is very sensitive to temperature, so do not use warm or ice cold water. Warm water will send the yeast into a frenzy, while ice cold water will shock it frozen, making it inactive. Mixing dough by hand won't heat the dough up much, but if you're using a machine you may need to cool the water to compensate for heat caused by friction. On the other hand, in winter, water from the tap is ice cold and may need warming slightly.

Then we slowly introduce the water to the flour. This is where the fun begins. The starch in the flour swells as it absorbs the water and creates the familiar texture of dough. The proteins bind together and form the strands of gluten. The yeast becomes part of the dough and has access to all the sugars in the flour.

The matter of when to add the salt is fiercely debated among pizza chefs. Some strongly believe that the salt kills the yeast and so it should be added at the end, while others disagree, arguing that they're eventually going to be mixed and spend hours together anyway. We err on the side of caution and add the salt near the end of mixing. It doesn't take much effort, so why not?

Kneading is a vital step for the dough – working the gluten strands into strong networks and creating strength and elasticity. Just like exercising our own muscles, the more we stretch and stress the gluten, the stronger it becomes. It takes around 8–10 minutes to work enough gluten for Neapolitan pizza. More than that and it becomes too tough and firm, so try not to over-knead.

The end result will be a silky-smooth mass of dough. It should be tenacious and elastic, but still soft and relaxed.

FERMENTATION

Fermentation happens when we allow the yeast enough time to work its magic. Time is crucial here. The more time, the more fermentation. The more fermentation, the more flavour is developed. We allow a lot of time for our dough in the pizzeria, at least 48 hours to be precise, in a process known as double fermentation. However, at home a single overnight fermentation for your dough will still produce a great end product.

Single Fermentation

Divide your dough into individual dough balls: 230g (8oz) for a 10-inch pizza or 260g (9oz) for a 12-inch

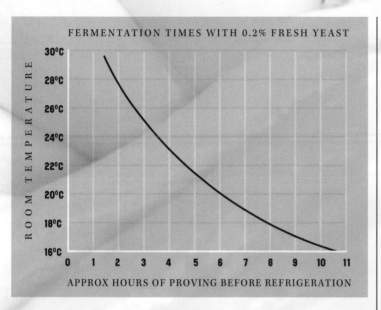

FERMENTATION TIMES WITH 0.2% FRESH YEAST

Fig iv. **Dough fermentation times with 0.2% fresh yeast**

pizza. Place these in a flat tray or container which you can seal airtight, or cover with clingfilm (plastic wrap). Leave your dough balls to ferment. Ideally place them somewhere with a consistent ambient temperature, as close to 20⁰C/68⁰F as possible. Avoid direct sunlight or anywhere with moving air. With our yeast at 0.2% of flour weight it should take approximately 6 hours for the dough to expand to almost double its original size, depending on room temperature. Refer to Fig iv for temperature vs hours for exact timings.

At this point, place the dough balls into the fridge to rest for at least another 18 hours. They can happily remain in the fridge for up to 2 days. It's the extra patience that goes a long way. The dough balls must be brought back to room temperature before making pizza. Cold dough is no good, since the yeast is asleep and the gluten is stiff. We need the yeast to wake up and the gluten to relax before cooking. So remove your dough from the fridge 2 hours before you want to cook it.

Double Fermentation

For those who want to take it to the next level, this method will extend the fermentation even further to maximise flavour. The first fermentation gives the yeast time to access all the starch from the flour and begin breaking it down. The second fermentation then enhances the flavour developed during the first fermentation and shapes the dough in preparation to make pizza.

This time, do not portion the dough into balls immediately. Instead, leave it as a whole or in 'bulk' in a container big enough to allow some expansion. The container must be airtight with a lid or sealed with clingfilm (plastic wrap). Let the dough rest like this overnight at ambient temperature.

The next morning divide your dough into individual

dough balls (see sizing for 'single fermentation'), knocking out the air and reworking each of them back into a tight ball. Place the dough balls in a flat tray or container which you can seal airtight, or cover with clingfilm. Leave these to ferment again for approximately 6 hours for the dough to expand to almost double its original size. Refer to Fig iv for exact timings.

Place them into the fridge to rest at least overnight. They can happily remain in the fridge for up to 2 days. The dough balls must be brought back to room temperature before making pizza. Cold dough is no good, since the yeast is asleep and the gluten is stiff. We need the yeast to wake up and the gluten to relax before cooking. So remove your dough from the fridge 2 hours before you want to cook it. By now, the dough should be at least 48 hours fermented before you make pizza.

Our resident dough man, Mr. Mullin.

The Pizza Pilgrims Recipes

Here it is, our greatest hits of pizza that we have featured on the menu at Pizza Pilgrims. This is basically the culmination of eight years of obsessing about pizza. Enjoy!

MAKİNG NEAPOLİTAN PİZZA DOUGH

With the knowledge of each ingredient and the important roles they play (see pages 92–95), we can now make Neapolitan pizza dough.

Tip: Weigh out all your ingredients before you start.

INGREDIENTS

1000g (35oz) '00' flour
(we recommend Caputo 'blue')

2g (⅔tsp) fresh yeast

620ml (21fl oz) tepid water

30g (1oz) fine sea salt

METHOD

1. Make a mountain of flour in the middle of the table. Using your fist, make a deep well in the middle of the flour, exposing the surface of the table (turning your mountain into a moon crater).

2. Crumble the yeast into the tepid water. Use your good hand to mash up the yeast in the water until it has dissolved. (Keep the other hand dry for taking Instagram photos to show off to your friends.) Fill your crater of flour with a third of the yeast/water mix. Using your fingertips, start making very small circular motions to combine the flour and water.

3. Start dragging in some more flour to the mix, by 'undercutting' the walls of the crater with your fingertips. As you do this the mixture in the middle will become thicker. Once it reaches the consistency of porridge you need to add a bit more water. Don't let it get too thick; if it starts to form a dough too soon it becomes difficult to incorporate the rest of the water. Keep dragging in a little flour to thicken the mix, then pouring a little bit more water in to loosen it, until you have used up all the water.

4. Sprinkle the sea salt over the mixture while it's still very wet to ensure it dissolves and disperses evenly throughout the dough. Now use both hands to push the remaining flour from the outside into the middle. Fold and press the mix until all the flour is absorbed and a dough comes together. If you have a dough scraper it really helps get everything off the table, but you can improvise with a paint scraper, spatula or knife.

5. Work the gluten by kneading the dough. Use the heel of your hand to stretch out the dough and roll it back up, while the other hand acts like an anchor. You'll be able to see the strands of gluten stretching, breaking, being put back together and becoming stronger. Continue this for about 8 minutes until the dough becomes smooth and glossy. It should also feel tighter and elastic.

6. Let the dough have a 10-minute rest to relax the gluten. Cover the dough with a damp cloth or some clingfilm (plastic wrap) to keep the air from drying it out. Then divide your bulk of dough into individual portions. We recommend 230g (8oz) dough balls for 10-inch pizzas. Ensure your dough balls are neatly shaped – pinched at the bottom and tight on the top – then place them in a tray or container 3cm (1in) apart. Cover with a tight lid or clingfilm (plastic wrap).

7. Now you can relax. The yeast will take over from here. Leave the dough at room temperature for approximately 6 hours until it expands to almost double its size, then store in the fridge overnight. The next day remove the dough from the fridge for 1–2 hours and bring it back to room temperature before making your pizzas.

STRETCHING YOUR OWN PIZZA BASE

Want to look like a boss when making pizza at home? That's what we thought. This is the traditional Neapolitan technique, in which you *have* to use your hands (a rolling pin is an absolute no-no). So, roll up your sleeves, dust your hands with flour like a gymnast stepping up to the parallel bars and channel your inner *pizzaiolo*.

1. Place your dough ball on a lightly floured surface then generously dust with more '00' flour. The dough ball should be completely covered in flour, as you don't want any sticky spots.

2. Using your fingertips, press out the dough ball firmly, starting at the centre and working your way out to the edges. It's important that this motion is a 'push down' and not a 'stretch out'. As you push out to the edges, leave the last inch of the dough untouched. This will become your crust.

3. Turn the dough over and repeat the process. The aim is to end up with a circle of dough about half the size of the final pizza, with a thin middle and a raised crust.

4. Transfer the pizza base to the back of your hands. The edge of the crust should rest on your knuckles, with the rest of the base hanging down. (It's a good idea to 'de-bling' just before this stage, as jewellery will poke a hole in the delicate dough.)

5. Now start stretching the dough between your hands. Try to stretch the outside edge, rather than the centre, as it will become too thin. Keep rotating the pizza base until you have arrived back where you started. Now you should have a 10-inch (ish) pizza base with a raised crust and a beautifully thin middle. If you hold it up to a light you should almost be able to see through it.

Fixing holes

If you over-stretch your dough and it gets too thin, you can end up with little holes in your pizza base. Just squeeze these back together before you put any toppings on. Easy.

Stuck pizzas

Try to move quickly with the dough, as it can stick to the work surface if left too long. If you're generous with the flour and add more during the process, you shouldn't end up in a sticky situation.

FRYING PAN PIZZA

We totally believe that making pizza using our frying pan (skillet) pizza method makes for the absolute best Neapolitan pizza you can make at home. Follow these simple steps below and we're sure you'll agree with us.

1.
Turn on your grill (broiler) to its highest setting and place an ovenproof frying pan (skillet) over a high heat. Grab your dough.

2.
Stretch out the pizza base following the instructions on page 101.

3.
Once your pizza base is about 10 inches wide, lay it in the hot, dry frying pan.

4.
Add the tomato sauce, Parmesan, basil, mozzarella and olive oil (in that order).

5.
When the base of the pizza has some colour and the crust has risen slightly, put the pan on the highest shelf under the hot grill.

6.
When the crust has tuned slightly golden and it has some good char bubbles your pizza is ready to eat!

TOP TIPS

- Before you start, place your frying pan (skillet) on the heat, turn your grill (broiler) on and place your oven shelf on the top rung – the hotter the better with this method.

- Use a wide-based ovenproof frying pan (skillet). Please don't melt any plastic handles!

- The olive oil goes on the pizza – not in the pan!

PIZZA IN THE POST

PIZZA PILGRIMS

In Spring 2020, we came up with a brand new way to deliver pizza – in the post! We post out our twice-proved dough and topping ingredients, then you get all the glory of making the pizza yourself at home!

THE KİT İNCLUDES:

- 2 x double fermented dough balls
- Our signature tomato sauce
- Fior di latte mozzarella
- Fresh basil
- Grated Parmesan
- Olive oil
- Caputo '00' flour, for dusting

ALL YOU'LL NEED İS:

- A grill (broiler)
- A wide-based, ovenproof frying pan (skillet)

So, if you fancy making Neapolitan pizza at home (but you don't want to get your hands *too* dirty), grab yourself one of our kits at www.pizzainthepost.co.uk and follow James' cook-along video! (UK only).

Share your creations with us @pizzapilgrims using #pizzainthepost and we'll rate your pizza!

Margherita

Where pizza all began... we can still remember the first time we tried a proper Neapolitan Margherita in Da Michele in Naples while on our Pizza Pilgrimage. The mozzarella had been made that day and was perfect. The combination of the light, charred pizza dough, sweet tomatoes, aromatic basil, peppery olive oil, savoury Parmesan and the milky white, creamy and slightly acidic mozzarella, just creates the most perfect flavour balance, which is the reason that the Margherita is the undisputed heavyweight champion of pizza. It is always the pizza that any pizza chef would order to get the measure of a new pizzeria because there is nothing to hide behind; no snazzy flavours to mask the quality of your ingredients, dough and skill in the oven.

FOR THE TOMATO SAUCE

Makes enough for 4 pizzas
1 x 400g (14oz) can of San Marzano (or any good-quality Italian) tomatoes
a good pinch of sea salt

METHOD

In a large bowl, crush the tomatoes by hand. (This is the old-school way they used to do it in Naples, and for good reason. If you put the tomatoes in a food processor you end up with a depressingly smooth sauce that lacks texture.) Once you've crushed the hell out of your tomatoes, add a pinch of salt to taste and that's it! Pure, unadulterated tomato goodness.

FOR THE PİZZA

1 ball of Neapolitan pizza dough (see page 100)
80g (3oz) tomato sauce (see left)
4–5 fresh basil leaves
Parmesan, for grating
1 tbsp olive oil
80g (3oz) fior di latte mozzarella, torn or sliced

METHOD

1. Preheat the grill (broiler) to its absolute highest setting, and place a large, ovenproof frying pan (skillet) over a high heat and let it get screaming hot.

2. Meanwhile, flatten and stretch the dough ball (following the instructions on page 101) to make a 10-inch pizza base.

3. Lay the pizza base flat in the hot, dry frying pan, then, using a small ladle (or a large spoon), spoon the tomato sauce onto the middle of the pizza. Using the back of the ladle, make concentric circles to spread the sauce, beginning in the middle and finishing 1½in from the edge.

4. Next, sprinkle over the basil (it will burn if put on last). Grate over a little Parmesan and drizzle with the olive oil.

5. Once the base of the pizza has browned, about 1–2 minutes, add your mozzarella, then place the frying pan under the grill on the highest shelf.

6. Once the crust has taken on some colour, about 1–2 minutes, the pizza is ready!

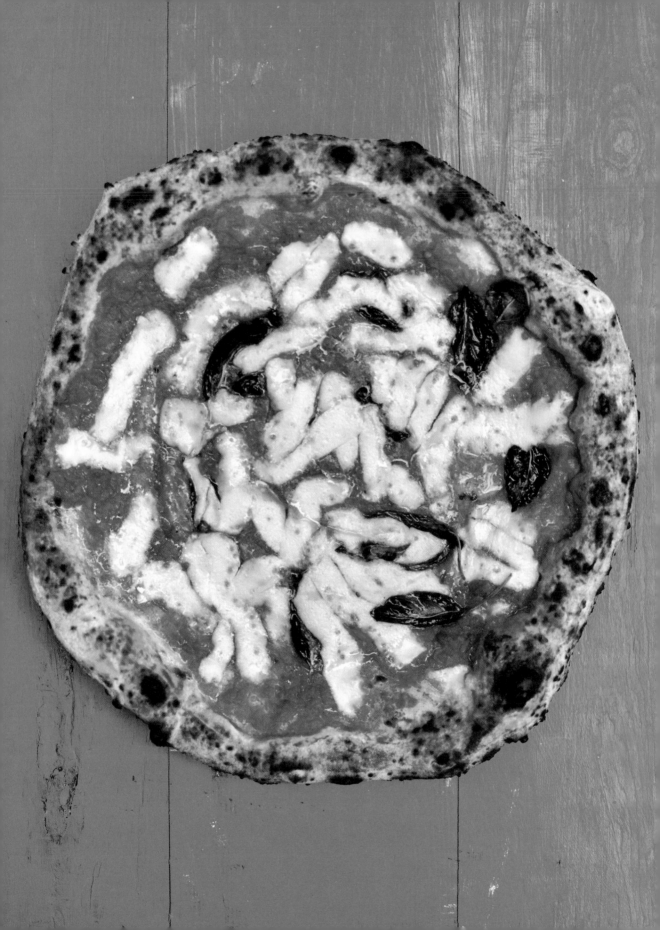

Marinara

The Marinara precedes even the Margherita. It's so called because it was the dish that was cooked for the fishermen of Naples when they came in off the boats. They did not have a lot of money to spend on food, so this flatbread topped with local tomatoes, garlic, olive oil and dried oregano became a local favourite. For us, the Marinara is the definition of 'punching above its weight' because, to be fair, it does at first glance look like a slightly naked Margherita. Do not underestimate the combo of garlic and herbs, though, because as soon as you take a bite you are smacked with a huge flavour punch. When this pizza is made right, it is pretty hard to beat.

INGREDIENTS

1 ball of Neapolitan pizza dough (see page 100)

140g (5oz) tomato sauce (see page 104)

½ garlic clove, finely sliced

1 tbsp good-quality olive oil

4–5 basil leaves

a good pinch of dried oregano

METHOD

1. Preheat the grill (broiler) to its absolute highest setting, and place a large, ovenproof frying pan (skillet) over a high heat and let it get screaming hot.

2. Meanwhile, flatten and stretch the dough ball (following the instructions on page 101) to make a 10-inch pizza base.

3. Lay the pizza base flat in the hot, dry frying pan, then, using a small ladle (or a large spoon), spoon the tomato sauce onto the middle of the pizza. Using the back of the ladle, make concentric circles to spread the sauce, beginning in the middle and finishing 1½in from the edge.

4. Top the pizza with the garlic slices, olive oil and basil. Once the base of the pizza has browned, about 1–2 minutes, place the frying pan under the grill on the highest shelf.

5. Once the crust has taken on some colour, about 1–2 minutes, remove the pizza from the grill and sprinkle with the dried oregano.

Bufala

The only thing cooler than ordering a Margherita in a Neapolitan pizzeria is ordering a bufala (and preferably adopting a strong Italian accent while wildly gesticulating with your hands – go on try it now… makes you feel good, right?). Neapolitans are intensely proud of their fior di latte, but the Mozzarella Di Bufala Campana is both DOC and DOP protected in Italy (essentially the more acronyms a product has after its name the posher it is – a lot like people, really). The mozzarella made using the milk from water buffalo has a higher fat content and therefore more flavour. We prefer to tear buffalo mozzarella instead of slicing it, as it keeps more of the milk in the cheese. The only real debate is whether it should be added before or after the pizza is cooked. Before means you get a beautiful melty stretch to the mozzarella, but after protects more of its delicate milkiness. Or just do what we do, and do both…

INGREDIENTS

1 ball of Neapolitan pizza dough (see page 100)

80g (3oz) tomato sauce (see page 104)

4–5 basil leaves

Parmesan, for grating

1 tbsp good-quality olive oil

80g (3oz) buffalo mozzarella, torn into pieces

METHOD

1. Preheat the grill (broiler) to its absolute highest setting, and place a large, ovenproof frying pan (skillet) over a high heat and let it get screaming hot.

2. Meanwhile, flatten and stretch the dough ball (following the instructions on page 101) to make a 10-inch pizza base.

3. Lay the pizza base flat in the hot, dry frying pan, then, using a small ladle (or a large spoon), spoon the tomato sauce onto the middle of the pizza. Using the back of the ladle, make concentric circles to spread the sauce, beginning in the middle and finishing 1½in from the edge. Then add the basil, a grating of Parmesan and the olive oil.

4. Once the base of the pizza has browned, about 1–2 minutes, add the mozzarella, then place the frying pan under the grill on the highest shelf for 1–2 minutes until the crust has taken on some colour. Or, make the pizza more like a Marinara (page 106) then top with cold, fresh buffalo mozzarella. (Or do both!)

Double Pepperoni & Spicy Honey

Spicy honey on pizza is an idea that we borrowed from our good friend Paulie Gee, of Paulie Gee's pizzeria in Greenpoint, NYC. Along with his first head chef, Mike, he created the Hellboy, a Marg topped with sopressata picante sausage and hot honey made by Mike. Mike ended up moving on from Paulie Gee's and starting Mike's Hot Honey, which is hands down the best spicy honey there is. We took this idea and put our own spin on it by adding two different types of pepperoni. We tried to import Mike's honey from the US but, after two failed attempts in which cases of honey got incinerated at customs (don't ask), we decided to create our own.

INGREDIENTS

1 ball of Neapolitan pizza dough
(see page 100)

80g (3oz) tomato sauce (see page 104)

4–5 basil leaves

Parmesan, for grating

1 tbsp good-quality olive oil

30g (1oz) each of 2 different types of sliced pepperoni

1 fresh chilli, sliced

80g (3oz) fior di latte mozzarella, torn or sliced

FOR THE SPICY HONEY

Makes enough for 10 pizzas

40g (1½oz) fresh chilli, sliced

100ml (scant ½ cup/3½fl oz) honey

METHOD

1. First, make the spicy honey by adding the chilli to the honey and leaving it to develop (at least 12 hours, but it keeps for up to 3 weeks).

2. Preheat the grill (broiler) to its absolute highest setting, and place a large, ovenproof frying pan (skillet) over a high heat and let it get screaming hot.

3. Meanwhile, flatten and stretch the dough ball (following the instructions on page 101) to make a 10-inch pizza base.

4. Lay the pizza base flat in the hot, dry frying pan, then, using a small ladle (or a large spoon), spoon the tomato sauce onto the middle of the pizza. Using the back of the ladle, make concentric circles to spread the sauce, beginning in the middle and finishing 1½in from the edge. Then add the basil, a grating of Parmesan, the olive oil, pepperoni and fresh chilli.

5. Once the base of the pizza has browned, about 1–2 minutes, add the mozzarella, then place the frying pan under the grill on the highest shelf.

6. Once the crust has taken on some colour, about 1–2 minutes, drizzle with some spicy honey and eat.

Smoked Napoli

This pizza still confuses us but we love it. It essentially involves putting all the saltiest ingredients on one pizza! We don't really understand how but the result is not overly salty. It's magic really. We use meaty smoked anchovies in oil that have a deep flavour, but you can use regular anchovy fillets if you like. Try to find tiny Lilliput capers that pop in your mouth, and the tiny purple olives that have a great savouriness to them. This is probably the most divisive pizza on our menu but also has the most loyal fans. ALWAYS drink with ice-cold beer.

INGREDIENTS

1 ball of Neapolitan pizza dough
(see page 100)

80g (3oz) tomato sauce (see page 104)

4–5 basil leaves

Parmesan, for grating

1 tbsp good-quality olive oil

3 smoked anchovy fillets

1 tsp capers

9 pitted black olives

80g (3oz) fior di latte mozzarella, torn or sliced

a good pinch of dried oregano

METHOD

1. Preheat the grill (broiler) to its absolute highest setting, and place a large, ovenproof frying pan (skillet) over a high heat and let it get screaming hot.

2. Meanwhile, flatten and stretch the dough ball (following the instructions on page 101) to make a 10-inch pizza base.

3. Lay the pizza base flat in the hot, dry frying pan, then, using a small ladle (or a large spoon), spoon the tomato sauce onto the middle of the pizza. Using the back of the ladle, make concentric circles to spread the sauce, beginning in the middle and finishing 1½in from the edge, then add the basil, a grating of Parmesan and the olive oil. Split the anchovy fillets lengthways with your fingers and drape over the pizza, then top with the capers and olives.

4. Once the base of the pizza has browned, about 1–2 minutes, add the mozzarella, then place the frying pan under the grill on the highest shelf.

5. Once the crust has taken on some colour, about 1–2 minutes, sprinkle with the dried oregano and eat.

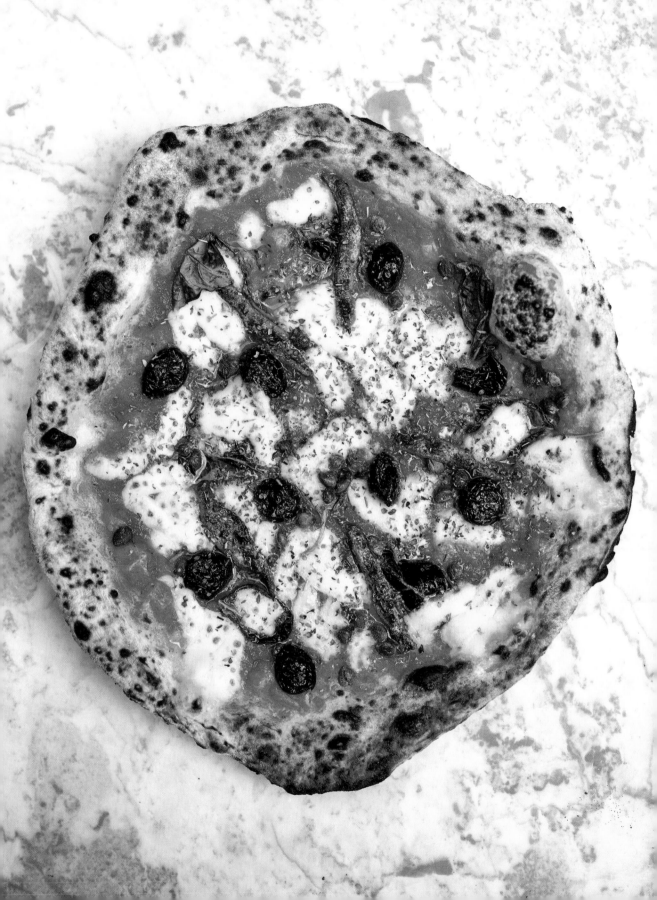

Neapolitan Salami & Fire-roasted Peppers

Neapolitan salami is quite specific when it comes to pizza. It has to have a coarse grain to it, whole black peppercorns in it, and it must be cut into matchsticks, not slices. This massively increases the surface area and means you get more flavour from less salami. We pair the salty salami with sweet, fire-roasted bell peppers.

INGREDIENTS

60g (2oz) Napoli black pepper salami

1 ball of Neapolitan pizza dough (see page 100)

80g (3oz) tomato sauce (see page 104)

4–5 basil leaves

Parmesan, for grating

1 tbsp good-quality olive oil

40g (1½oz) roasted bell peppers (either jarred or roasted whole over the hob at home)

80g (3oz) fior di latte mozzarella, torn or sliced

METHOD

1. To prepare your salami, cut into slices 3–4mm (⅙–⅛in) thick, then stack the slices like coins and slice into 3–4mm (⅙–⅛in) matchsticks.

2. Preheat the grill (broiler) to its absolute highest setting, and place a large, ovenproof frying pan (skillet) over a high heat and let it get screaming hot.

3. Meanwhile, flatten and stretch the dough ball (following the instructions on page 101) to make a 10-inch pizza base.

4. Lay the pizza base flat in the hot, dry frying pan, then, using a small ladle (or a large spoon), spoon the tomato sauce onto the middle of the pizza. Using the back of the ladle, make concentric circles to spread the sauce, beginning in the middle and finishing 1½in from the edge, then add the basil, a grating of Parmesan and the olive oil. Tear your roasted peppers into bite-sized chunks and place evenly over the pizza, then top with the salami matchsticks.

5. Once the base of the pizza has browned, about 1–2 minutes, add the mozzarella, then place the frying pan under the grill on the highest shelf.

6. Once the crust has taken on some colour, about 1–2 minutes, your pizza is ready!

Aubergine Parmigiana

We wanted a pizza on the menu that would be both vegetarian and a real comfort food hit. The one dish that makes all our pizzaioli go weak at the knees, except pizza, is aubergine parmigiana. So, we put it on a pizza.

FOR THE PARMİGİANA

Makes enough for 5 pizzas

2 aubergines (eggplant), cut into 2cm/¾in cubes

3 garlic cloves, finely chopped

100ml (scant ½ cup) good-quality olive oil

50g (1¾oz) tomato paste

2 x 400g (14oz) cans good-quality peeled plum tomatoes

100ml (scant ½ cup) water

a small handful of basil leaves

salt and freshly ground black pepper

FOR THE PİZZA

1 ball of Neapolitan pizza dough (see page 100)

4–5 basil leaves

Parmesan, for grating, plus 5g (⅛oz) shavings to finish

1 tbsp good-quality olive oil, plus extra for drizzling

25g (1oz) cherry plum tomatoes

80g (3oz) fior di latte mozzarella, torn or sliced

METHOD

1. First, toss the aubergine cubes in salt in a colander set over a bowl and leave for at least an hour. Preheat your oven to 250°C/480°F/ Gas 10.

2. Add your garlic and olive oil to a large, ovenproof saucepan and place over a medium heat. Slowly cook until the garlic is golden brown.

3. Dry the aubergine cubes with a clean cloth, then add them to the pan and cook until the aubergine has softened.

4. Stir in the tomato paste and cook for a further 3 minutes, then add the canned tomatoes and water. Place in the hot oven (with the lid off), stirring occasionally for 30–40 minutes until the sauce has reduced and the aubergine is soft and tender. Season with salt and pepper to taste and leave to cool.

5. Preheat the grill (broiler) to its absolute highest setting, and place a large, ovenproof frying pan (skillet) over a high heat and let it get screaming hot.

6. Meanwhile, flatten and stretch the dough ball (following the instructions on page 101) to make a 10-inch pizza base.

7. Lay the pizza base flat in the hot, dry frying pan, then spread over 100g (3½oz) of the aubergine parmigiana. Top with the basil, a grating of Parmesan, the tablespoon of olive oil and cherry tomatoes.

8. Once the base of the pizza has browned, about 1–2 minutes, add the mozzarella, then place the frying pan under the grill on the highest shelf.

9. Once the crust has taken on some colour, about 1–2 minutes, finish the cooked pizza with the Parmesan shavings and a drizzle of olive oil.

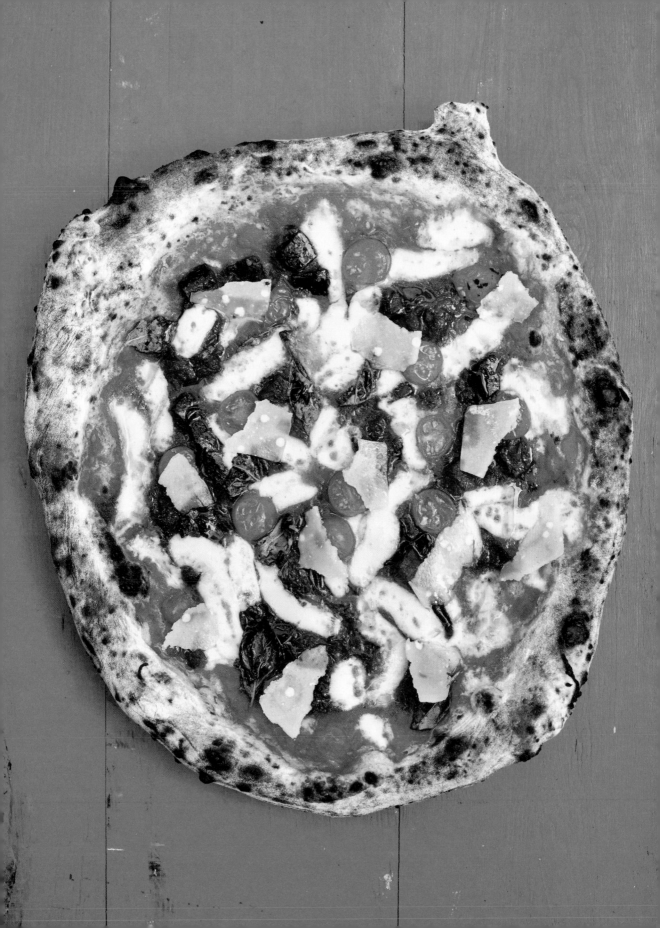

Salsiccia e Friarielli

Things that Neapolitan chefs treasure: Maradona, good espresso, Nutella, their mums... and *salsiccia e friarielli*. This is one of the true flavours of a Naples kitchen. On the face of it, it's just two ingredients: coarse-ground Italian pork sausage and a special type of local wild broccoli called *friarielli*, which is fried in olive oil, garlic and chilli. It can be served as antipasti, or mixed into pasta or risotto. The best way to eat it, though, is on pizza.

FOR THE SALSICCIA E FRIARIELLI

Makes enough for 5 pizzas
olive oil, for cooking
6 big fat Italian pork sausages
2 large garlic cloves, finely sliced
a good pinch of chilli flakes
400g (14oz) fresh or frozen friarielli (use tenderstem broccoli if you can't find it)
a splash of white wine
salt and freshly ground black pepper

METHOD

1. Place a deep frying pan on a medium heat and add a glug of olive oil. Add the whole sausages into the pan and fry for about 5 minutes, until they take on some colour.

2. Add your garlic and chilli flakes and fry for a further 30 seconds, then add your friarielli.

3. Add the wine and simmer for 10–15 minutes until the wine has cooked off, the friarielli is tender and the sausages are cooked all the way through. Remove from the heat, season to taste and set aside to cool. When cool, remove the sausages and cut into chunks.

FOR THE PIZZA

1 ball of Neapolitan pizza dough (see page 100)
155g (5½oz) salsiccia e friarielli (see left)
Parmesan, for grating
1 tbsp good-quality olive oil
sliced fresh chilli, to taste
80g (3oz) smoked mozzarella, torn or sliced

METHOD

1. Preheat the grill (broiler) to its absolute highest setting, and place a large, ovenproof frying pan (skillet) over a high heat and let it get screaming hot.

2. Meanwhile, flatten and stretch the dough ball (following the instructions on page 101) to make a 10-inch pizza base.

3. Lay the pizza base flat in the hot, dry frying pan, then spread the salsiccia e friarielli evenly across the base. Grate over some Parmesan, drizzle over a little olive oil and scatter on the fresh chilli slices.

4. Once the base of the pizza has browned, about 1–2 minutes, add the smoked mozzarella, then place the frying pan under the grill on the highest shelf.

5. Once the crust has taken on some colour, about 1–2 minutes, your pizza is ready!

’Nduja

We are writing this page from Calabria, the home of ’nduja, having just returned from visiting our ’nduja supplier, Vincenzo, who showed us around his factory. The passion for ’nduja in Calabria is huge. It's a style of pork sausage which is made from the fattiest parts of the pig: the cheeks and the belly. The meat is minced finely with salt, Calabrian chillies and a mix of herbs and spices, including fennel and black pepper. It is then kneaded like dough to create an amazing paste which is unceremoniously stuffed into a pig's intestine. From there, the sausage is smoked and cured to mature the flavour. The result is a soft, cured paste that is packed with flavour and fiery heat. Used as a pizza topping it is an absolute winner.

INGREDIENTS

1 ball of Neapolitan pizza dough (see page 100)

80g (3oz) tomato sauce (see page 104)

4–5 basil leaves

Parmesan, for grating

1 tbsp good-quality olive oil

60g (2oz) ’nduja sausage

80g (3oz) fior di latte mozzarella, torn or sliced

METHOD

1. Preheat the grill (broiler) to its absolute highest setting, and place a large, ovenproof frying pan (skillet) over a high heat and let it get screaming hot.

2. Meanwhile, flatten and stretch the dough ball (following the instructions on page 101) to make a 10-inch pizza base.

3. Lay the pizza base flat in the hot, dry frying pan, then, using a small ladle (or a large spoon), spoon the tomato sauce onto the middle of the pizza. Using the back of the ladle, make concentric circles to spread the sauce, beginning in the middle and finishing 1½in from the edge. Then add the basil, a grating of Parmesan and the olive oil. Pinch off pieces of the ’nduja and scatter over the pizza.

4. Once the base of the pizza has browned, about 1–2 minutes, add the mozzarella, then place the frying pan under the grill on the highest shelf.

5. Once the crust has taken on some colour, about 1–2 minutes, your pizza is ready!

Carbonara

We wanted to pay homage to this pasta heavy-hitter by creating its pizza cousin. Carbonara pizza had been done before but in a very anglicised way, with cream and cooked ham... We wanted to stay true to the authentic traditions, which means using guanciale (cured pig's cheek) and, of course, NO cream! As mentioned in Divisive Ingredients (page 72), this pizza caused some scandal with our customers. Pasta on pizza is a pizza purist's no-no, but we found ourselves between a rock and hard place – be authentic to carbonara pasta or be authentic to pizza. It really came down to tasting, and carbonara pizza with bucatini pasta on top is *definitely* better... but we do offer it with no pasta to keep everyone happy.

INGREDIENTS

1 ball of Neapolitan pizza dough (see page 100)

50g (1¾oz) cooked and cooled bucatini pasta

Parmesan, for grating

80g (3oz) fior di latte mozzarella, torn or sliced

60g (2oz) diced guanciale (or pancetta if easier), cooked until golden

1 tbsp good-quality olive oil

1 egg yolk, broken up with a fork

freshly ground black pepper

METHOD

1. Preheat the grill (broiler) to its absolute highest setting, and place a large, ovenproof frying pan (skillet) over a high heat and let it get screaming hot.

2. Meanwhile, flatten and stretch the dough ball (following the instructions on page 101) to make a 10-inch pizza base.

3. Lay the pizza base flat in the hot, dry frying pan then drape over the pasta (reserving a few strands). Top with a grating of Parmesan, the mozzarella, guanciale and the olive oil. Add a few more strands of pasta, then drizzle the whole pizza with the egg yolk.

4. Once the base of the pizza has browned, about 1–2 minutes, place the frying pan under the grill on the highest shelf.

5. Once the crust has taken on some colour, about 1–2 minutes, generously season with lots of black pepper and eat.

Roast Mushroom & Truffle

One of the great Italian flavour combinations, mushroom and truffle were made for each other. We used to serve this pizza simply using thinly sliced mushrooms, like most pizzerias. But we wanted a deeper mushroom flavour so we developed a technique of roasting the sliced mushrooms in the oven with olive oil, garlic, pepper and salt. Lots of mushroom liquor, which is full of flavour, runs out of the mushrooms so we use a little flour to thicken the liquid to create an intensely flavourful mushroom ragu that we spoon over the base. Once cooked, we top it with a drizzle of white truffle oil from Alba.

INGREDIENTS

1 ball of Neapolitan pizza dough
(see page 100)

4–5 basil leaves

Parmesan, for grating

1 tbsp good-quality olive oil

80g (3oz) fior di latte mozzarella, torn or sliced

1 tbsp white truffle oil

FOR THE MUSHROOM MIXTURE

Makes enough for 4 pizzas

100ml (scant ½ cup) good-quality olive oil

4 garlic cloves, finely chopped

500g (1lb 2oz) chestnut mushrooms, finely sliced

a good pinch of salt

1 tbsp plain (all-purpose) flour

METHOD

1. First make the mushroom mixture by heating the olive oil and garlic gently in a saucepan. Allow the garlic to turn golden before adding the sliced mushrooms and salt. Fry until the mushrooms have softened and their liquid has been released.

2. Take off the heat, tilt the mushrooms to one side of the pan and collect the mushroom juices in the other side of the pan. Stir the flour into the liquid until smooth and put back on the heat. Stir continuously until you have a thick liquor coating the mushrooms. Leave to cool.

3. Preheat the grill (broiler) to its absolute highest setting, and place a large, ovenproof frying pan (skillet) over a high heat and let it get screaming hot.

4. Meanwhile, flatten and stretch the dough ball (following the instructions on page 101) to make a 10-inch pizza base.

5. Lay the pizza base flat in the hot, dry frying pan, then spread with some mushroom mixture. Top with the basil, a grating of Parmesan and the olive oil.

6. Once the base of the pizza has browned, about 1–2 minutes, add the mozzarella, then place the frying pan under the grill on the highest shelf.

7. Once the crust has taken on some colour, about 1–2 minutes, drizzle with the truffle oil and eat.

Capricciosa

The translation of the word capricciosa tells you everything you need to know about this pizza and why it is such a menu staple; the word directly translates as 'capricious', which the Oxford dictionary defines as: 'Given to sudden and unaccountable changes of mood and behaviour'. Amazing. Who doesn't know a fickle pizza orderer who incessantly claims, 'I don't know what to have!'? This pizza solves that problem because it is basically topped with every ingredient in the pizzaiolo's arsenal. You can order this pizza safe in the knowledge that you will not experience pizza FOMO or orderer's remorse.

INGREDIENTS

1 ball of Neapolitan pizza dough
(see page 100)

80g (3oz) tomato sauce (see page 104)

4–5 basil leaves

Parmesan, for grating

1 tbsp good-quality olive oil

35g (1¼oz) chargrilled artichokes
(in oil, from a jar)

50g (1¾oz) prosciutto cotto

40g (1½oz) mushroom mixture (see page 124)

30g (1oz) black olives

80g (3oz) fior di latte mozzarella, torn or sliced

a good pinch of dried oregano

METHOD

1. Preheat the grill (broiler) to its absolute highest setting, and place a large, ovenproof frying pan (skillet) over a high heat and let it get screaming hot.

2. Meanwhile, flatten and stretch the dough ball (following the instructions on page 101) to make a 10-inch pizza base.

3. Lay the pizza base flat in the hot, dry frying pan, then, using a small ladle (or a large spoon), spoon the tomato sauce onto the middle of the pizza. Using the back of the ladle, make concentric circles to spread the sauce, beginning in the middle and finishing 1½in from the edge. Then add the basil, a grating of Parmesan and the olive oil. Top with the artichokes, prosciutto cotto, mushroom mixture and olives.

4. Once the base of the pizza has browned, about 1–2 minutes, add the mozzarella, then place the frying pan under the grill on the highest shelf.

5. Once the crust has taken on some colour, about 1–2 minutes, scatter with dried oregano and eat.

Fiorentina

It was actually the French who first coined the phrase *a la Florentine*, to describe dishes featuring spinach, cheese and egg. It's not known why, but eggs Florentine is a breakfast staple the world over. With that logic it can be deduced that pizza fiorentina is a perfect breakfast pizza to be eaten without shame or guilt (although all pizzas are breakfast pizzas, right?). Our version of this green goddess of a pizza was developed by our very own head chef Tom Mullin, a Northern Irish lad with a penchant for good Irish butter.

INGREDIENTS

a large knob of butter

200g (7oz) spinach leaves, finely shredded

80g (3oz) double (heavy) cream

¼ tsp freshly grated nutmeg

Parmesan, for grating

1 ball of Neapolitan pizza dough
(see page 100)

80g (3oz) fior di latte mozzarella, torn or sliced

1 egg yolk

sea salt and cracked black pepper

METHOD

1. First melt the knob of butter in a pan, then fill the pan with the spinach. Wait until it has wilted down then add the cream, nutmeg, and some salt and pepper to taste. Cook down for a few minutes, remove from the heat and grate in some Parmesan to taste. Leave to cool.

2. Preheat the grill (broiler) to its absolute highest setting, and place a large, ovenproof frying pan (skillet) over a high heat and let it get screaming hot.

3. Meanwhile, flatten and stretch the dough ball (following the instructions on page 101) to make a 10-inch pizza base.

4. Lay the pizza base flat in the hot, dry frying pan, then spread with the spinach mixture. Add the mozzarella and some more grated Parmesan, then gently place the egg yolk in the centre of the pizza.

5. Once the base of the pizza has browned, about 1–2 minutes, place the frying pan under the grill on the highest shelf.

6. Once the crust has taken on some colour, about 1–2 minutes, finish with some cracked black pepper.

Americano

In the years following World War II there was a wave of Americanisation that swept across southern Italy. It was immortalised in the 1956 jazz hit *Tu Vuò Fà L'Americano* ('You want to be an American'), which sung about a Neapolitan man who wanted to live like an American, drinking whisky and soda, dancing to rock and roll, playing baseball and smoking Camel cigarettes. This pizza is an ode to the love of American culture and has a place in the traditional Neapolitan pizza line-up. An absolute favourite among kids, the pizza is essentially a Margherita topped with French fries and sliced-up Frankfurters. In short: It. Is. Delicious. But it is not one your doctor would like you eating.

INGREDIENTS

1 ball of Neapolitan pizza dough (see page 100)

80g (3oz) tomato sauce (see page 104)

4–5 basil leaves

Parmesan, for grating

1 tbsp good-quality olive oil

60g (2oz) Frankfurter sausage, sliced

80g (3oz) fior di latte mozzarella, torn or sliced

80g (3oz) cooked fries

tomato ketchup, to serve

METHOD

1. Preheat the grill (broiler) to its absolute highest setting, and place a large, ovenproof frying pan (skillet) over a high heat and let it get screaming hot.

2. Meanwhile, flatten and stretch the dough ball (following the instructions on page 101) to make a 10-inch pizza base.

3. Lay the pizza base flat in the hot, dry frying pan, then, using a small ladle (or a large spoon), spoon the tomato sauce onto the middle of the pizza. Using the back of the ladle, make concentric circles to spread the sauce, beginning in the middle and finishing 1½in from the edge. Then add the basil, a grating of Parmesan, the olive oil and the sliced Frankfurter sausage.

4. Once the base of the pizza has browned, about 1–2 minutes, add the mozzarella, then place the frying pan under the grill on the highest shelf.

5. Once the crust has taken on some colour, about 1–2 minutes, scatter the fries over the top and serve with ketchup.

Datterini Filetti

The celebration of tomatoes, mozzarella and basil on a pizza is where it all began, and this pizza makes a slight twist on the Margherita, with dramatic effect. By switching out the pulped San Marzano tomato for little sliced datterini tomatoes you completely change the flavour of the pizza. The tomatoes have a sweet acidity that you don't get in a tomato sauce, and when you bite into them, they pop, giving you an explosion of tomato flavour. This is the ultimate summer pizza, and feels light and refreshing like a tomato salad. To take this pizza to the next level, top with a whole burrata before serving. Naughty.

INGREDIENTS

1 ball of Neapolitan pizza dough (see page 100)

80g (3oz) pesto

4–5 basil leaves

Parmesan, for grating

1 tbsp good-quality olive oil, plus extra to finish

80g (3oz) baby datterini tomatoes, sliced

a pinch of salt

80g (3oz) fior di latte mozzarella, torn or sliced

whole burrata (optional)

METHOD

1. Preheat the grill (broiler) to its absolute highest setting, and place a large, ovenproof frying pan (skillet) over a high heat and let it get screaming hot.

2. Meanwhile, flatten and stretch the dough ball (following the instructions on page 101) to make a 10-inch pizza base.

3. Lay the pizza base flat in the hot, dry frying pan, then spread with the pesto. Next add the basil, a grating of Parmesan and the olive oil.

4. Toss the sliced tomatoes in a pinch of salt.

5. Once the base of the pizza has browned, about 1–2 minutes, add the mozzarella and tomatoes, then place the frying pan under the grill on the highest shelf.

6. Once the crust has taken on some colour, about 1–2 minutes, top with a whole burrata (if using) and drizzle with some more olive oil.

Gianfranco GorgonZola

This was a rare opportunity to celebrate two things that we love: creamy Gorgonzola blue cheese from Milan and the Italian football legend and nineties star of London's Chelsea Football Club, Gianfranco Zola. Much like its namesake, this pizza has an explosive energy, great strength and an understanding of the offside rule that is unrivalled (hang on – this analogy is beginning to fall over…). Truth be told, it's just a great pun but is nonetheless a delicious pizza. We pair this with an Italian wheat beer, and it's a hell of a combo.

INGREDIENTS

1 small courgette (zucchini)

1 ball of Neapolitan pizza dough (see page 100)

4–5 basil leaves

60g (2oz) sweet Gorgonzola, in small pieces

Parmesan, for grating

1 tbsp good-quality olive oil

80g (3oz) fior di latte mozzarella, torn or sliced

a good pinch of dried oregano

METHOD

1. Using a speed/swivel peeler, create courgette ribbons by running the peeler lengthways down the courgette. You need about 50g (1¾oz).

2. Preheat the grill (broiler) to its absolute highest setting, and place a large, ovenproof frying pan (skillet) over a high heat and let it get screaming hot.

3. Meanwhile, flatten and stretch the dough ball (following the instructions on page 101) to make a 10-inch pizza base.

4. Lay the pizza base flat in the hot, dry frying pan, then scatter over the basil leaves and courgette ribbons. Top with the Gorgonzola, a grating of Parmesan and the olive oil.

5. Once the base of the pizza has browned, about 1–2 minutes, add the mozzarella, then place the frying pan under the grill on the highest shelf.

6. Once the crust has taken on some colour, about 1–2 minutes, scatter with some dried oregano and eat.

Mimosa

Another favourite of the kids of Naples, everything about this pizza screams comfort. Think of it like the Neapolitan equivalent of the British fish fingers, chips and baked beans supper. The mimosa is actually a little yellow flower which is given to women on International Women's Day. We serve this pizza each March to celebrate the female pizzaiolas in our company and IWD. The Italians flock to buy it but, oddly, Londoners tend to turn their nose up at it (they are missing out!).

INGREDIENTS

1 ball of Neapolitan pizza dough (see page 100)

40ml (1¼fl oz) double (heavy) cream

4–5 basil leaves

Parmesan, for grating

1 tbsp good-quality olive oil

80g (3oz) fior di latte mozzarella, torn or sliced

2 slices of good-quality Italian roasted ham

2 tbsp canned sweetcorn (corn)

cracked black pepper

METHOD

1. Preheat the grill (broiler) to its absolute highest setting, and place a large, ovenproof frying pan (skillet) over a high heat and let it get screaming hot.

2. Meanwhile, flatten and stretch the dough ball (following the instructions on page 101) to make a 10-inch pizza base.

3. Lay the pizza base flat in the hot, dry frying pan, then spread with the double cream. Add the basil, a grating of Parmesan and the olive oil, then top with the mozzarella, ham and sweetcorn.

4. Once the base of the pizza has browned, about 1–2 minutes, place the frying pan under the grill on the highest shelf.

5. Once the crust has taken on some colour, about 1–2 minutes, finish with some cracked black pepper.

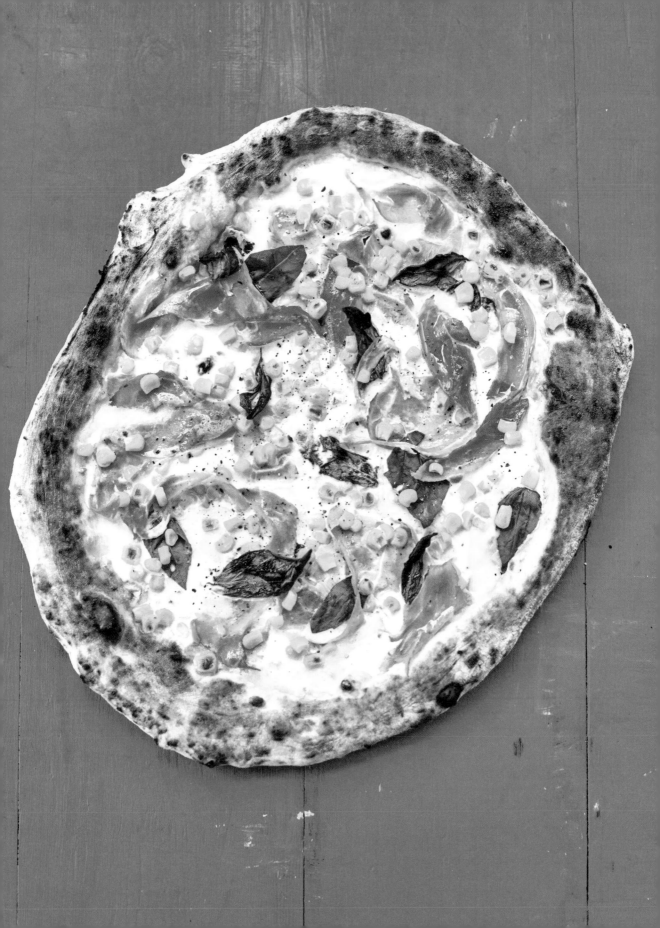

Mortadella & Pistachio

Mortadella originates in Bologna (AKA 'The Fat City') and is the ham of choice for sandwiches, or panini, across the whole of Italy. It is made by finely mincing pork and incorporating 15% small cubes of pork back fat; our favourite style includes whole toasted pistachios from Bronte in Sicily. We use a pistachio butter (like peanut butter but with pistachios... we know, KNOCK OUT!) to spread across the base of the pizza and cook with mozzarella, Parmesan and basil. We top the cooked pizza with mortadella and spoons of stracciatella (the creamy centre of a burrata). The nuttiness of the pistachio butter, with the saltiness of the mortadella and the cool creaminess of the cheese, is one of our favourite ever combos.

INGREDIENTS

1 ball of Neapolitan pizza dough (see page 100)

40g (1½oz) pistachio butter, let down with 20ml (4 tsp) water

4–5 basil leaves

Parmesan, for grating

1 tbsp good-quality olive oil

60g (2oz) fior di latte mozzarella, torn or sliced

3 slices of mortadella

60g (2oz) burrata or buffalo mozzarella, torn into pieces

30g (1oz) pistachios, lightly toasted and roughly chopped

METHOD

1. Preheat the grill (broiler) to its absolute highest setting, and place a large, ovenproof frying pan (skillet) over a high heat and let it get screaming hot.

2. Meanwhile, flatten and stretch the dough ball (following the instructions on page 101) to make a 10-inch pizza base.

3. Lay the pizza base flat in the hot, dry frying pan, then spread with the pistachio butter. Add the basil, a grating of Parmesan and the olive oil.

4. Once the base of the pizza has browned, about 1–2 minutes, add the mozzarella, then place the frying pan under the grill on the highest shelf.

5. Once the crust has taken on some colour, about 1–2 minutes, top the pizza with the mortadella, burrata and toasted pistachios.

Pumpkin, Sausage, Sage & Chilli

This pizza was inspired by the first man to teach us how to make pizza – Gianluca. He was our cooking teacher when we were in Tuscany and he made a pumpkin and sausage pasta dish that we will remember for ever. We took this recipe as gospel and just transported it onto a pizza, which in our opinion sums up the taste of autumn perfectly.

INGREDIENTS

1 ball of Neapolitan pizza dough
(see page 100)

Parmesan, for grating

1 tbsp good-quality olive oil

80g (3oz) fior di latte mozzarella, torn or sliced

60g (2oz) roasted fennel sausage, cut into bite-sized pieces

4–5 sage leaves

sliced fresh chilli, to taste

chilli oil, to serve

FOR THE PUMPKIN MIXTURE

Makes enough for 4 pizzas

40g (1½oz) butter

50ml (scant ¼ cup) good-quality olive oil

2 garlic cloves, finely diced

500g (1lb 2oz) diced pumpkin
(prepared weight)

salt and freshly ground black pepper

METHOD

1. For the pumpkin, heat the butter, oil and garlic in a large saucepan until the garlic is golden brown. Tip in the pumpkin and cook, stirring occasionally, on a medium heat until soft. Add salt and pepper to taste, then take off the heat and leave to cool.

2. Preheat the grill (broiler) to its absolute highest setting, and place a large, ovenproof frying pan (skillet) over a high heat and let it get screaming hot.

3. Meanwhile, flatten and stretch the dough ball (following the instructions on page 101) to make a 10-inch pizza base.

4. Lay the pizza base flat in the hot, dry frying pan, then spread with 80g (3oz) of the pumpkin mixture. Grate over some Parmesan and drizzle with the olive oil, then top with the mozzarella, sausage, sage leaves and fresh chilli.

5. Once the base of the pizza has browned, about 1–2 minutes, place the frying pan under the grill on the highest shelf.

6. Once the crust has taken on some colour, about 1–2 minutes, drizzle with chilli oil.

Porchetta & Poponcini Peppers

Porchetta, surely the Rolls Royce of Italian hams (or maybe it's more the Humvee?), is originally from a small town called Ariccia, 16 miles south-east of Rome. A suckling pig is completely deboned and sprinkled with a number of things, including salt, lemon zest, rosemary, garlic, fennel seeds, chilli and black pepper. It is then rolled and trussed with string before being slow-cooked over a spit. After about eight hours the skin becomes the most incredible crackling and the meat melt-in-the-mouth tender. Poponcini peppers have an incredible sweet-and-sour flavour, while giving a little heat. This pizza is testament to the benefits of simplicity. Two flavours together on a pizza, perfectly balanced.

INGREDIENTS

1 ball of Neapolitan pizza dough
(see page 100)

80g (3oz) tomato sauce (see page 104)

4–5 basil leaves

Parmesan, for grating

1 tbsp good-quality olive oil

80g (3oz) fior di latte mozzarella, torn or sliced

80g (3oz) thinly sliced porchetta,
torn into pieces

60g (2oz) sweet Gorgonzola, in small pieces

40g (1½oz) drained poponcini peppers

METHOD

1. Preheat the grill (broiler) to its absolute highest setting, and place a large, ovenproof frying pan (skillet) over a high heat and let it get screaming hot.

2. Meanwhile, flatten and stretch the dough ball (following the instructions on page 101) to make a 10-inch pizza base.

3. Lay the pizza base flat in the hot, dry frying pan, then, using a small ladle (or a large spoon), spoon the tomato sauce onto the middle of the pizza. Using the back of the ladle, make concentric circles to spread the sauce, beginning in the middle and finishing 1½in from the edge. Then add the basil, a grating of Parmesan, the olive oil and mozzarella. Top with the porchetta, Gorgonzola and poponcini peppers.

4. Once the base of the pizza has browned, about 1–2 minutes, place the frying pan under the grill on the highest shelf.

5. Once the crust has taken on some colour, about 1–2 minutes, your pizza is ready!

Calzone Ripieno

The calzone can be traced back as far as the Margherita and perhaps even further, when bread dough was stuffed, folded and then deep-fried – AKA pizza fritta (see page 54), which is the calzone's deep-fried brother (and arguably even more delicious). For our calzone we stick to the Naples traditions. The flavour is completely different to normal pizza because the dough protects the ingredients from the fire of the oven and instead steams them, giving a more delicate flavour.

INGREDIENTS

1 x 260g (9oz) ball of Neapolitan pizza dough (see page 100)

40g (1½oz) ricotta

80g (3oz) fior di latte mozzarella, torn or sliced

60g (2oz) tomato sauce (see page 104)

Parmesan, for grating

30g (1oz) mushroom mixture (see 124)

60g (2oz) Napoli salami

4–5 basil leaves

1 tbsp good-quality olive oil

METHOD

1. Preheat your oven to its highest temperature. Meanwhile, flatten and stretch the dough ball (following the instructions on page 101) to make a 12-inch pizza base, *without* a pronounced crust.

2. Spread the ricotta over one half of the base. Top with half the mozzarella, then half the tomato sauce, a grating of Parmesan, all of the mushrooms and salami, half the basil and half the olive oil.

3. Fold the un-topped half of the pizza over the topped half and, using your fist, hammer down on the edges to create a tight seal. Use your finger to gently tear a small hole in the top of the calzone to let steam out.

4. Top the pizza with the remaining ingredients and a grating of Parmesan, to create a Margherita pizza on top.

5. Bake in the hot oven until the calzone is golden and charred.

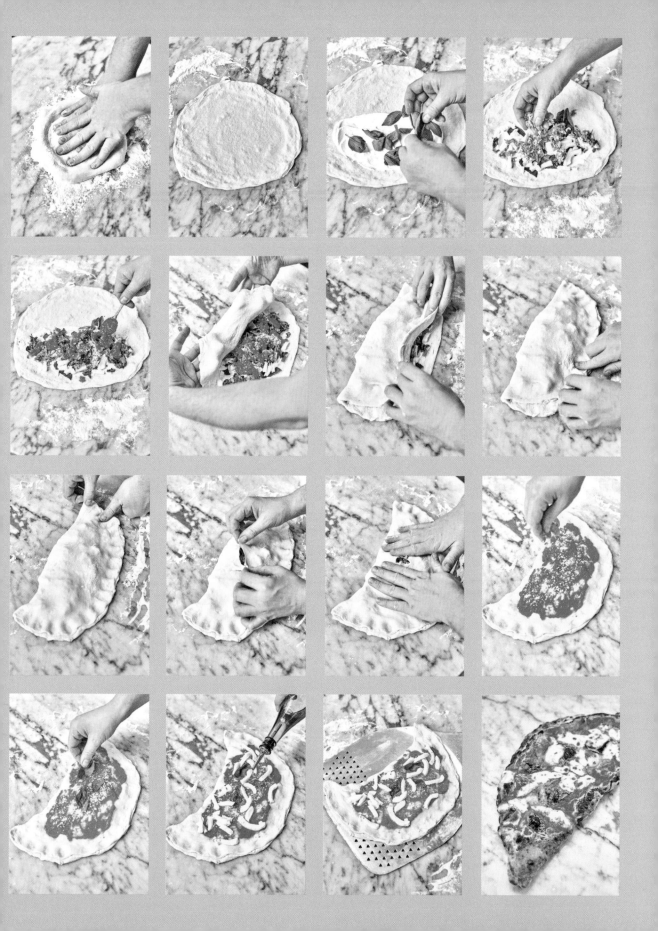

Kale, Anchovy & Chilli

Pizza in January: a battle for the newly health-conscious trying to stick to their New Year's resolutions. So we decided to create a pizza choice on our menu called 'Heaven or Hell'. Two pizzas you could choose from that would send you to heaven or hell. The Americano featured on page 130 played the part of hell and this pizza was the virtuous heaven. Kale's superfood status aside, this is a great combo of earthy anchovy and kale flavours with buffalo mozzarella and a kick of heat from the chilli. We promise it won't disappoint, and it's good for you (ish…), so happy days!

INGREDIENTS

1 ball of Neapolitan pizza dough
(see page 100)

80g (3oz) buffalo mozzarella,
torn into pieces

Parmesan, for grating

sliced fresh chilli, to taste

1 tbsp good-quality olive oil

chilli oil, to serve

FOR THE KALE AND ANCHOVY

Makes enough for 1 pizza

30g (1oz) kale leaves, roughly sliced

1 tbsp good-quality olive oil

1 garlic clove, chopped

3 anchovy fillets in oil

METHOD

1. Blanch the kale leaves in boiling, salted water for 2–3 minutes until tender, then drain and plunge the leaves into ice-cold water (to retain the colour).

2. Heat the olive oil and garlic in a frying pan until the garlic begins to turn golden. Add the anchovy fillets and cook until they melt into the oil. Add in the drained kale and cook on a medium heat until the kale has taken on all the oil. Take off the heat and leave to cool.

3. Preheat the grill (broiler) to its absolute highest setting, and place a large, ovenproof frying pan (skillet) over a high heat and let it get screaming hot.

4. Meanwhile, flatten and stretch the dough ball (following the instructions on page 101) to make a 10-inch pizza base.

5. Lay the pizza base flat in the hot, dry frying pan then top with 100g (3½oz) of the kale mix, the mozzarella, Parmesan, fresh chilli and olive oil.

6. Once the base of the pizza has browned, about 1–2 minutes, place the frying pan under the grill on the highest shelf.

7. Once the crust has taken on some colour, about 1–2 minutes, drizzle with chilli oil.

Pizza Fiocco

This pizza was invented by Roberto Sustra and his brother, who together run a little pizzeria outside of Naples, in Vomero. He starts with slices of ham on a pizza base, a drizzle of double cream and then uses a potato ricer to 'snow' fine stands of what is essentially mashed potato all over the pizza. He then finishes with grated Parmesan, olive oil and black pepper. As it cooks it creates a beautiful crispy top like a rosti, with a thin layer of light and fluffy potato underneath. If pizza was a hug, this would be it.

INGREDIENTS

1 large potato, peeled
1 ball of Neapolitan pizza dough
(see page 100)
35ml (2½ tbsp) double (heavy) cream
3 slices of prosciutto crudo
80g (3oz) fior di latte mozzarella, torn or sliced
Parmesan, for grating
1 tbsp good-quality olive oil
freshly ground black pepper

METHOD

1. Start by boiling the potato until tender, then drain.

2. Preheat the grill (broiler) to its absolute highest setting, and place a large, ovenproof frying pan (skillet) over a high heat and let it get screaming hot.

3. Meanwhile, flatten and stretch the dough ball (following the instructions on page 101) to make a 10-inch pizza base.

4. Lay the pizza base flat in the hot, dry frying pan, then pour over the cream.

5. Drape the prosciutto slices flat on the base and top with the mozzarella.

6. Using a potato ricer, rice the potato onto the pizza to create one even 'duvet' of a layer that covers the prosciutto.

7. Finish with a generous grating of Parmesan, a drizzle of olive oil and some cracked black pepper.

8. Once the base of the pizza has browned, about 1–2 minutes, place the frying pan under the grill on the highest shelf.

9. Once the crust has taken on some colour, about 1–2 minutes, your hug-in-a-pizza is ready!

Burrata Diavola

We're going to completely come clean here. This was a pizza invented out of necessity, like all good things, right? We'd teamed up with Samsung to create a secret menu for their customers. But, we have to admit, that we completely forgot and 30 minutes before they were about to turn up and taste the creation we had spent so long(!) developing, James was in the kitchen trying to knock something together with the ingredients we had! Starting with a Margherita, he went down a meat lover's angle using our pepperoni and 'nduja, then topped the whole thing off with a mini burrata, our spicy honey and fresh chilli slices. It was a quick fix, but has gone on to be one of our best-selling pizzas. Sorry Team Samsung, if you're reading this… but it all worked out in the end – Bob Dylan wrote *Blowin' in the Wind* in 10 minutes, right?! (Disclaimer: We would like to make it clear that in no way are we comparing a swanky pepperoni pizza to a seminal protest anthem – we just got a little carried away….)

INGREDIENTS

1 ball of Neapolitan pizza dough (see page 100)

80g (3oz) tomato sauce (see page 104)

4–5 basil leaves

Parmesan, for grating

1 tbsp good-quality olive oil

60g (2oz) 'nduja, ripped into 5–6 blobs

50g (1¾oz) sliced pepperoni

sliced fresh chilli, to taste

80g (3oz) fior di latte mozzarella, torn or sliced

a mini 50g (1¾oz) burrata

spicy honey (see page 110), for drizzling

METHOD

1. Preheat the grill (broiler) to its absolute highest setting, and place a large, ovenproof frying pan (skillet) over a high heat and let it get screaming hot.

2. Meanwhile, flatten and stretch the dough ball (following the instructions on page 101) to make a 10-inch pizza base.

3. Lay the pizza base flat in the hot, dry frying pan, then, using a small ladle (or a large spoon), spoon the tomato sauce onto the middle of the pizza. Using the back of the ladle, make concentric circles to spread the sauce, beginning in the middle and finishing 1½in from the edge. Then add the basil, a grating of Parmesan and the olive oil. Top evenly with the 'nduja pieces, pepperoni slices and fresh chilli.

4. Once the base of the pizza has browned, about 1–2 minutes, add the mozzarella, then place the frying pan under the grill on the highest shelf.

5. Once the crust has taken on some colour, about 1–2 minutes, place a mini burrata in the centre and drizzle with spicy honey.

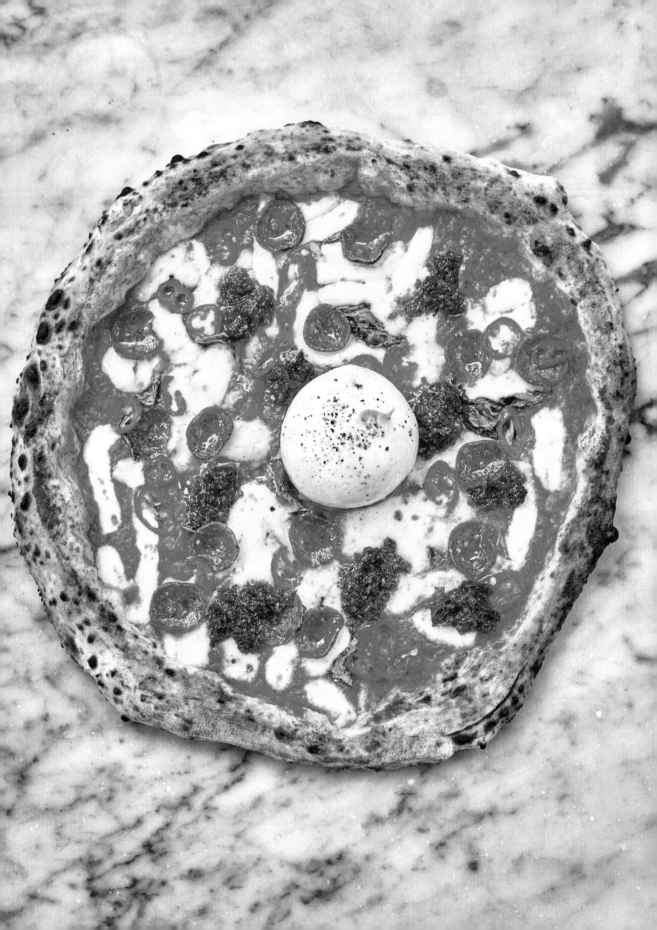

Prosciutto Crudo, Rocket & Parmesan

OK, so we've had time to think about it. Porchetta is definitely the Humvee of hams, leaving the Rolls Royce spot free for infinitely elegant Prosciutto di Parma DOC. We challenge you to add a few thin slices of this amazing cured meat to any pizza and not make it more delicious! We were lucky enough to visit the Prosciutto di Parma factory on our Pizza Pilgrimage and see the painstaking detail that goes into creating this world-renowned ingredient. This pizza is an ode to the Italian classic flavour combo of these three ingredients.

INGREDIENTS

1 ball of Neapolitan pizza dough (see page 100)

80g (3oz) tomato sauce (see page 104)

4–5 basil leaves

Parmesan, for grating, plus 15g (½oz) shavings, to serve

1 tbsp good-quality olive oil, plus extra to finish

80g (3oz) fior di latte mozzarella, torn or sliced

a small handful of rocket (arugula) leaves

3–4 slices of prosciutto crudo

METHOD

1. Preheat the grill (broiler) to its absolute highest setting, and place a large, ovenproof frying pan (skillet) over a high heat and let it get screaming hot.

2. Meanwhile, flatten and stretch the dough ball (following the instructions on page 101) to make a 10-inch pizza base.

3. Lay the pizza base flat in the hot, dry frying pan, then, using a small ladle (or a large spoon), spoon the tomato sauce onto the middle of the pizza. Using the back of the ladle, make concentric circles to spread the sauce, beginning in the middle and finishing 1½in from the edge. Then add the basil, a grating of Parmesan and the tablespoon of olive oil.

4. Once the base of the pizza has browned, about 1–2 minutes, add the mozzarella then place the frying pan under the grill on the highest shelf.

5. Once the crust has taken on some colour, about 1–2 minutes, you have to act fast. Scatter over a bed of rocket, lay the prosciutto slices over the top, then finish by sprinkling the Parmesan shavings over everything and adding a good drizzle of olive oil.

Asparagus & Pancetta

In the UK we grow the most amazing fresh asparagus between the beginning of April and the end of June, and we wanted to celebrate these glorious British spears as best we could. Asparagus' best friend is a good smoky bacon, so we thought it was a great opportunity to marry up one of the UK's best ingredients with one of Italy's – smoked pancetta.

INGREDIENTS

5 asparagus spears

40g (1½oz) cubed smoked pancetta

1 ball of Neapolitan pizza dough (see page 100)

Parmesan, for grating, plus 15g (½oz) shavings, to serve

4–5 basil leaves

80g (3oz) fior di latte mozzarella, torn or sliced

FOR THE LEMON AND PARSLEY OIL

Makes enough for 5 pizzas

50ml (scant ¼ cup) good-quality olive oil

a small handful of chopped parsley

grated zest and juice of ½ lemon

METHOD

1. Start by prepping the asparagus. Snap the tough ends off the spears and discard. Using a swivel peeler, peel the bottom of the asparagus to get rid of any tough skin.

2. Take a high-sided saucepan and, using your asparagus spear as a guide, fill the pan up until only the head of the asparagus is out of the water. Bring to the boil, wrap all the asparagus spears together with an elastic band and place in the water so that only the heads stick out. This will boil the stems and steam the tops, meaning perfect asparagus every time. Once tender, drain and plunge into ice-cold water, to prevent over-cooking.

3. Heat the pancetta in a frying pan and slowly cook down until the fat has rendered out and the pancetta is golden brown.

4. For the lemon and parsley oil, stir together the olive oil, parsley and lemon zest and juice. Leave to infuse.

5. Preheat the grill (broiler) to its absolute highest setting, and place a large, ovenproof frying pan (skillet) over a high heat and let it get screaming hot.

6. Meanwhile, flatten and stretch the dough ball (following the instructions on page 101) to make a 10-inch pizza base.

7. Lay the pizza base flat in the hot, dry frying pan, then add a grating of Parmesan and the basil. Place the asparagus spears over the top and then scatter over the pancetta.

8. Once the base of the pizza has browned, about 1–2 minutes, add the mozzarella then place the frying pan under the grill on the highest shelf.

9. Once the crust has taken on some colour, about 1–2 minutes, drizzle with a tablespoon of the lemon and parsley oil and scatter with Parmesan shavings.

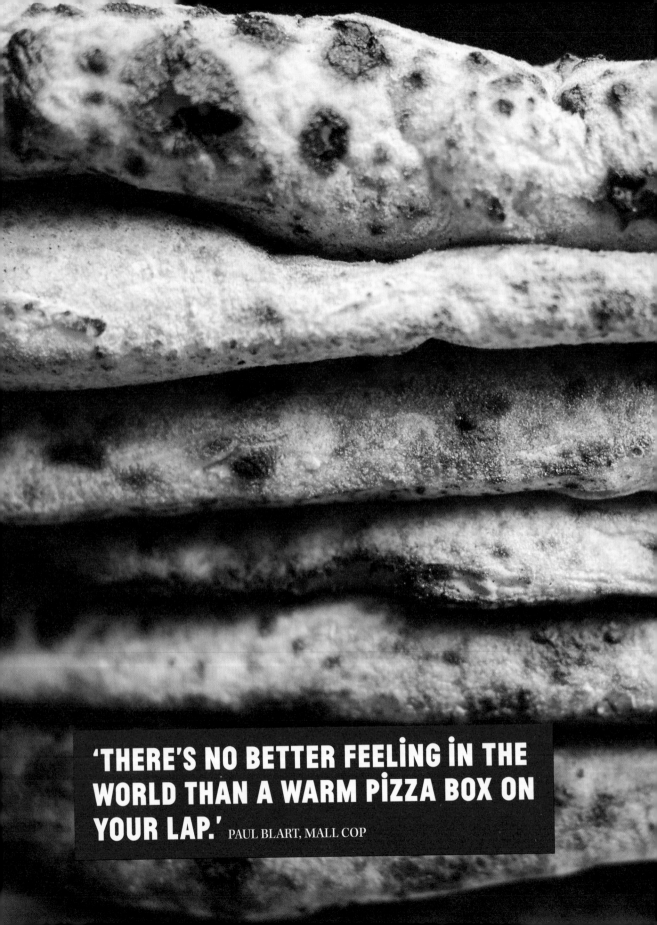

'THERE'S NO BETTER FEELING IN THE WORLD THAN A WARM PIZZA BOX ON YOUR LAP.' PAUL BLART, MALL COP

Pizza dudes at Forcella Pizza,
Lorimer, NYC.

Crust Dippers

A totally American invention that we have adopted in our pizzerias to help promote the love of the crust and to avoid the pizza cardinal sin of not eating your crusts. Here are five ideas for crust dippers you can make quickly and easily at home. But first things first, let's get a basic mayonnaise recipe down...

BASIC MAYO (AKA YOUR CRUST DIPPER FLAVOUR VEHICLE)

Add one or two egg yolks to a mixing bowl. Give it a quick whisk to break them up, then take a combo of neutral flavoured oil (we like sunflower) and enough extra-virgin olive oil to impart some flavour but without overpowering with bitter flavour. Begin to slowly trickle the oils into the bowl, whisking vigorously using a balloon whisk (add the oil very gradually to begin with as this is when the mayo is most likely to split). Once it starts to thicken, you can increase the flow of oil. You want to add enough oil so that when you pick up the whisk the mayo does not run off. This is to add maximum 'mayo grab' to the crust. Once you have your basic emulsion, add a little salt and pepper to taste; we also add a splash of lemon juice to give a little acidity. From here you have a blank canvas to make whatever crust dippers you want. Go for your life. Nothing is off limits.

WHITE TRUFFLE

For this you're going to have to hunt down your local Italian deli or maybe head online. In Italy they make an incredible '*crema di funghi con tartufo*', which is a slow-cooked mushroom paste with truffle. In the pizzerias we use this paste as a base by adding it to our mayo mix; the paste adds an amazing umami flavour as well as colour, with beautiful flecks of mushroom and truffle. To ramp up the truffle flavour, we then add extra white truffle oil to taste.

PESTO

If it's possible, this is even simpler. We use a fresh basil leaf pesto from our friends at Belazu to mix with our mayo base to make a thick, creamy pesto dipper that is hands down our best seller.

'NDUJA

This is one for the spicy meat lovers! We get hands-on by skinning an 'nduja, donning a pair of *Breaking Bad*-style gloves and massaging the 'nduja until we have a soft paste that has been slightly warmed by our hands and is therefore releasing some oils. We then add the mayo base and again massage the 'nduja into the mayo with our hands. The result is a bright red, deep, meaty and intensely flavoured 'nduja dipper.

SALSA VERDE

For this we don't use a mayo base but make a classic salsa verde. Take big bunches of all your favourite fresh herbs. We use basil, parsley, a little mint, fresh oregano and rosemary. To use the technical term: 'Chop the hell out of them' until you have really fine flecks of herbs. In a bowl, mix some good-quality olive oil, a couple of anchovy fillets that have been pulverised using the side of the knife, some chopped capers, grated lemon zest, salt and pepper and a little lemon juice. Add the herbs and combine until you have a thick mixture that is shiny and just drops off a spoon. Taste for seasoning and add more salt and lemon juice if it needs it. (FYI this is an awesome sauce to serve with chicken, fish, veggies... basically anything!)

ARRABBİATA

Heat some good-quality olive oil in a pan and chuck in a couple of whole, fat garlic cloves that have been smashed under the back of a knife. Sauté for a couple of minutes, then add as many chilli flakes as you dare. Cook for another minute, fish out the garlic cloves, then add a couple of cans of plum tomatoes. Lower the heat and cook until the tomatoes have reduced by at least a third and broken down to a smooth sauce. Check the seasoning and add salt and sugar to taste. Don't forget that when the sauce cools, the flavours will dull down slightly, so be bold! You can serve this hot too, but we think cold works best as a crust dipper.

PESTO

SALSA VERDE

'NDUJA

WHITE TRUFFLE

ARRABBIATA

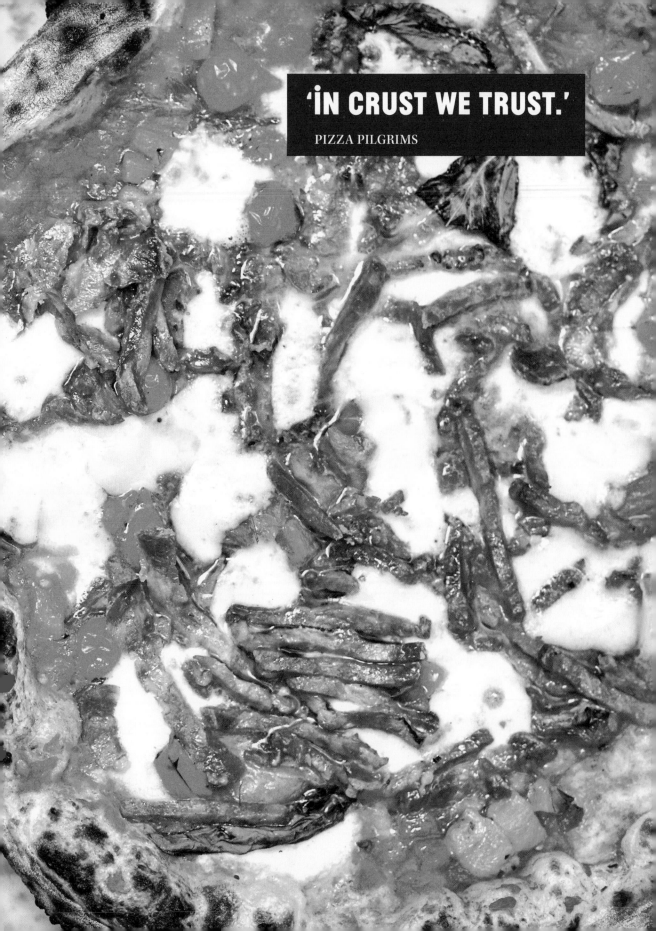

'IN CRUST WE TRUST.'

PIZZA PILGRIMS

Pizza Soup

Just bear with us…

When we opened our third pizzeria on London's Exmouth Market, we had the opportunity to re-establish a market stall outside our shop. We opened in the dead of winter – and we wanted to come up with something to 'warm the cockles' and which was linked to, but not exactly, pizza. Enter, pizza soup. Essentially a deconstructed pizza – the idea was a simple tomato and basil soup, served with individual mini mozzarella and Parmesan calzones. It was truly delicious and fun, as well as really easy to make. We kept the stall throughout the winter – but seemingly the world was not quite ready for pizza soup in 2015. Maybe now is its time!

FOR THE SOUP

Serves 2

3 garlic cloves, peeled

drizzle of good-quality olive oil

3 heaped tsp tomato paste

2 x 400g (14oz) cans chopped tomatoes

large pinch each of salt and sugar

2 large handfuls of basil leaves

FOR THE MİNİ CALZONE

1 ball of Neapolitan pizza dough (see page 100)

buffalo mozzarella

Parmesan, for grating

METHOD

1. Preheat your oven to its hottest setting.

2. Fry the garlic cloves in the olive oil in a large pan over a medium heat. After 3 minutes, add the tomato paste and cook, stirring, for 2 minutes, before adding the canned tomatoes. Add the salt and sugar, and simmer for 15 minutes. Taste and check for seasoning, then take off the heat and stir in the basil leaves.

3. While the soup is simmering, cut the dough ball in half and create a mini pizza base with each, following the method on page 101.

4. Tear off two or three bite-sized pieces of mozzarella per calzone and place on one half of the pizza bases.

5. Fold the bases in half, sealing around the edge, then grate some Parmesan over the top of each.

6. Bake in the oven for 10 minutes, or until taking on some colour.

7. Serve the soup in bowls with the mini calzone alongside.

Chilli Oil

Last summer we headed out to Calabria, the very southern tip of Italy and the spiritual home of Italian chilli. We took some of the team from our pizzerias to the annual Peperoncino Festival in Diamante. The goal of the trip was to get some first-hand experience of the 'high' that you feel when you eat lots of chilli.

The festival was mad. Hundreds of stalls lined the beach serving every single product or dish you could imagine, but laced with chilli. We started off slow but soon worked our way up to the big leagues when we found a guy selling what he called 'Calabrian Nutella'. He handed us a teaspoon of it and, once we'd eaten it, he told us it was pure Carolina Reaper chilli paste, with a cool 2.2 million on the Scoville heat scale. It hits you like a bus, and all of a sudden your mouth is on fire and you begin to panic. For about five minutes we were genuinely scared, but as the pain begins to plateau, and the rising fear of death begins to pass, you start to feel amazing! The rest of the evening was a bit of a blur but there is a video on our YouTube channel of the night, which is worth a watch.

When we got home, we wanted to create a chilli oil that would replicate this feeling, and this is the recipe we settled on. A really good kick but with the fruity flavour of the Carolina Reaper chilli, and garlic and smoked paprika for flavour.

İNGREDİENTS

Makes about 500ml/2 cups

500ml (generous 2 cups) good-quality, light olive oil

50g (1¾oz) garlic, very finely chopped

1 fresh Carolina Reaper chilli

50g (1¾oz) dried Calabrian chilli flakes

10g (⅓oz) smoked paprika

METHOD

1. Put the olive oil, garlic and the whole chilli (ensuring to prick with a knife so it doesn't explode on you!) in a saucepan.

2. Cook on a low heat until the garlic has gone a light golden brown and the chilli has softened.

3. Remove the pan from the heat and add the chilli flakes and smoked paprika.

4. Stir well and leave to cool. Decant into a clean bottle along with all of the bits in the pan, if possible. This chilli oil is good for use for up to 3 weeks.

The Nutella Ring

Nutella was invented in 1946 by Pietro Ferrero, who started adding hazelnuts to his chocolate in World War II to compensate for sugar rationing. It took him another 10 years to add lecithin to make his hazelnut chocolate spreadable – and he was off to the races. It is reported by the BBC that Nutella is now enjoyed in 160 countries, and 365 million kilos are devoured per year worldwide. That's a million kilos a day, or the weight of the Empire State Building, across the whole year.

Nutella is almost a way of life in Italy. Pretty much every single kid grows up eating Nutella with *cornetto* (croissant), *grissini* (breadsticks), in white bread sandwiches, on ice cream, and even in espresso.

At the pizzerias we make a Nutella and salted ricotta pizza ring that has been a best seller since the pizza-van days. We stretch out a long rectangle of pizza dough, then lay down a fat line of Nutella and ricotta. We finish with a sprinkle of sea salt just to up the addictiveness, then fold the dough over to create a Nutella stuffed snack. We then bring the ends together to make a ring and bake it in the pizza oven. It's served with a ball of vanilla gelato. Something about the salty dough and the sweet Nutella makes this criminally addictive!

INGREDIENTS

130g (4½oz) Neapolitan pizza dough
(see page 100)
40g (1½oz) ricotta
about 100g (3½oz) Nutella
sea salt
ice cream, to serve

METHOD

1. Preheat your oven as hot as it will go.
2. Using your fingertips, stretch out the dough into a long rectangle about 35cm/14in long and 12cm/5in wide.
3. Using a spoon, spread the ricotta over the dough lengthways in a long line. Then spoon as much Nutella as you can onto the dough in a long line down the middle of the ricotta. Sprinkle with sea salt.
4. Fold the dough over itself lengthways so you have a long Nutella parcel, then, using a closed fist, hammer the long edge to ensure a really strong seal on the dough.
5. Bring the ends of the parcel around to create a ring (with the seam on the inside) and press the two ends of dough together, using your fist again to make a strong seal.
6. Bake until the ring has inflated and the crust is golden. Serve with vanilla ice cream.

NUTELLA FUN FACTS

- Nutella buys 25% of the world's hazelnut supply every year: over 100,000 tons.

- Each 400g (14oz) jar of Nutella contains 52 hazelnuts.

- World Nutella Day is 5th February.

- In 2013, some sweet-toothed bandits pulled off a heist on a Nutella lorry, stealing 5 metric tonnes of the stuff, worth an estimated £20,000.

- Italy loves Nutella so much that in 2014 they commemorated it on a postage stamp. Does that make Nutella the Queen of Italy?!

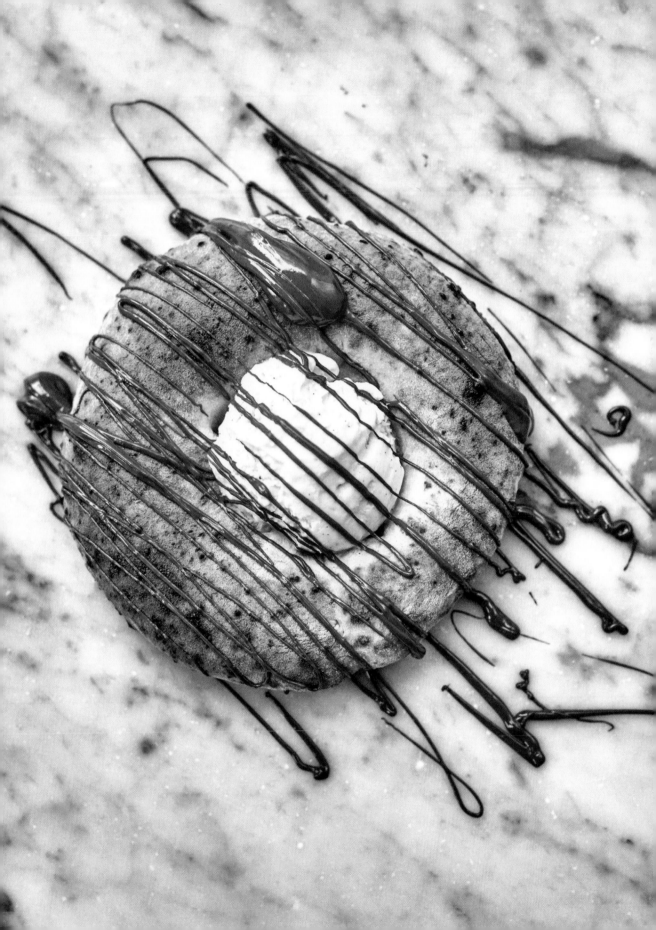

Calzonification

Yeah, it's a real word for sure.

kal.zone.if.ik.ay.she.un
verb. the act of wrapping chocolate bars in pizza dough and baking them in the oven.

In 2017, we opened our pizzeria in London's Shoreditch and were looking for a fun way to bring it to the attention of the local area. The Nutella Ring (see page 164) had long been a big part of our menu and, as such, we decided to explore what other chocolatey treats could be improved by wrapping them in dough. We made a short YouTube video about our exploits which got over 20 million views in just a couple of weeks. Fair to say we were on to something!

We experimented with a selection of chocolate bars and confectionery combinations, and here are a few of our findings:

MARS & REESE'S PIECES

Like a Snickers on speed, this melty, caramelly, nutty dream is guaranteed to make you happy (while shaving a few years off your life).

QUALITY STREET

This takes Forrest Gump's mum's famous quip about a box of chocolates and really ups the ante. Bite-sized morsels of chocolate with an element of surprise every single time. Brilliant fun.

CREME EGG

In a similar vein to the chip shops in the UK that will deep-fry a creme egg for you, the dough adds a salty layer to the famous Easter sugar hit, and elevates it to another level.

KINDER BUENO

The real game changer here is the crunch from the Bueno bar. To really spice this one up, throw in a couple of Kinder Surprise eggs to the mix (after you have taken the prizes out of course).

WARNING: HARIBO STAR MIX

We'd like to confirm that this combo doesn't work AT ALL. Pizza dough and Haribo should forever be kept apart. You heard it here first.

What to Drink with Pizza

Some tips for loading up that Globe bar at home...

Count Camillo Negroni, what a guy. From posh Italian stock, he consistently bucked tradition. Travelling across America, spending some time as a cowboy, then living in London, learning to love gin. He then headed home to his favourite bar, Caffè Casoni, in Florence, Italy in 1919. It was here he decided his Americano cocktail wasn't packing the punch, so he asked his bartender to strengthen it up by switching the soda for gin. It became an instant hit and is still one of the best ways to kick off a good night. Here's our recipe for the classic and a couple of twists to have a go at.

NEGRONI

The original and the best...

    25ml (1fl oz) Campari
    25ml (1fl oz) London dry gin
    25ml (1fl oz) Martini Rosso
    slice of orange, to garnish

Fill a whisky tumbler with ice. Pour over your alcohols and stir.

Add the orange garnish and drink. Make another...

'A NEGRONI IS A PERFECT DRINK AS FAR AS I'M CONCERNED... THAT FIRST SIP IS CONFUSING AND NOT PARTICULARLY PLEASANT. BUT MAN, IT GROWS ON YOU.'

ANTHONY BOURDAIN

NEGRONI BIANCO

This is the meekest and mildest of the negroni family. Perfect as a 'sundowner' cocktail while riding a giant inflatable swan across an infinity pool... we reckon.

  25ml (1fl oz) Cocchi Bianco vermouth

  25ml (1fl oz) London dry gin

  25ml (1fl oz) Luxardo Bitter Bianco liqueur

  twist of grapefruit peel, to garnish

Fill a whisky tumbler with ice. Pour over your alcohols and stir.

Add the grapefruit garnish and drink.

PEPPERGRONI

How do you go about making a negroni better? Well, we answered that age-old question by adding Bourbon and garnishing with pepperoni slices. Job done.

This is a slightly sweeter and smokier variation on the classic, so it's good for people who don't like the really bitter notes of negronis. And, of course, people who are just looking to get more pepperoni in their lives...

  25ml (1fl oz) Campari

  25ml (1fl oz) Knob Creek (or your favourite) Bourbon

  25ml (1fl oz) Martini Rosso

  3 slices of pepperoni on a cocktail stick, to garnish

Fill a whisky tumbler with ice. Pour over your alcohols and stir.

Add the pepperoni garnish and drink.

Limoncello

Limoncello can often fall into the same bracket as a holiday friendship – you make an acquaintance on a sunny beach somewhere and think, this is a lifelong friendship. Then you realise, when you are drinking it warm on a Tuesday night with take-out, that it's not as great as you thought it was.

That said, when not purchased in a bottle in the shape of a stiletto heel – or the shape of Italy – limoncello can be delicious. Really, truly, finish-off-the-bottle delicious. If you have ever been to Naples or the Amalfi coast, you know this to be true. And given it was invented around the bay of Naples, you can bet it goes well with a pizza!

Despite being the second favourite liqueur in Italy (after Campari) it has not really travelled the world to a great extent. It was this exact issue – the difficulty of getting hold of a good limoncello for the pizzerias – that led us to make our own, from amazing Amalfi lemons (sourced from the Aceto groves above the town of Amalfi) and award-winning Chase vodka from Herefordshire.

So, we guess our message here is, shop with caution. You are looking for a limoncello in a non-novelty bottle, with a pale yellow colour (not luminous) and an opaque liquid (highlighting a high level of lemon essential oil). It is also worth looking for one made with real Amalfi lemons – only these contain the full density of oil in the skins to make a great product. Just saying: our Pococello (pococello.com) ticks all the boxes!

What is also surprising is how versatile limoncello is...

LIMONCELLO SPRITZ

A great alternative to an Aperol Spritz, this is a super-refreshing (and super-Italian) way to while away those summer nights.

50ml (3 tbsp) good-quality limoncello

125ml (½ cup) prosecco

20ml (4 tsp) sparkling water

sprig of rosemary, to garnish

Pour over ice and serve with the rosemary.

LIMONCELLO & TONIC

This is a lower-ABV, sweeter version of a gin and tonic.

50ml (3 tbsp) good-quality limoncello

125ml (½ cup) tonic water

slice of lemon, to garnish

Serve over ice.

Luigi Aceto, the lemon man of Amalfi.

İCE-COLD LIMONCELLO SHOTS

One for the purist: this is the
original way to drink shots
(and happily the fastest).
Keep your limoncello
(and your shot glasses) in
the freezer and enjoy quickly!

Spritzes

APEROL SPRITZ

This has exploded out of Italy recently. It is huge in Venice, but its lurid orangey goodness is now just as comfortable on the streets of Shoreditch or Williamsburg. Try it straight with white wine rather than prosecco, or for a more grown-up version replace the Aperol with Campari. The classic way to serve this is as a 3, 2, 1:

3 parts prosecco (or white wine)

2 parts Aperol (or Campari)

1 part sparkling water

slice of orange, to garnish

Serve over ice.

ELDERFLOWER SPRITZ

Another classic Italian flavour profile recreated as a spritz – the classy choice!

50ml (3 tbsp) elderflower liqueur

125ml (½ cup) prosecco

25ml (scant 2 tbsp) sparkling water

slice of lemon, to garnish

Serve over ice.

CYNAR SPRITZ

We are keen to meet the person who decided to create a liqueur out of artichoke hearts – that must have been a very late-night plan. However, Cynar is actually delicious – albeit ferociously bitter. If you need to wimp out, dilute with prosecco!

50ml (3 tbsp) Cynar liqueur

125ml (½ cup) prosecco

25ml (scant 2 tbsp) sparkling water

Serve over ice.

Italian Beer

Italy has (like almost every nation on earth) really gone all-out on craft beers in the last few years. This from a country which, for all its amazing elegance, haute couture and style, still sees Tennent's Super as the height of sophistication (it will often be at the top of a beer list in a posh restaurant or swanky bar).

Anyway – there are many, many other better options available, and it seemed appropriate for pizza beer to be Italian. So here are a couple of our favourites...

BIRRA DEL BORGO

We visited this fantastic craft brewery, just outside of Rome, in 2015 on our second pilgrimage through Italy. They are lovely people – and genuinely come up with some fantastic (and completely off-the-wall) beers. We love the hoppy Reale, their Lisa lager is delicious and refreshing, and their constant wheel of creativity means there is always something new to try (oyster beer anyone?). The bottle is iconic also – we have served it in our pizzerias for almost five years now and it is universally loved.

BIRRA MORETTI

Not exactly a 'craft beer' – this lager brand has been owned by Heineken for many years and is growing fast. However, it is a great beer for food, and in our mind is a nicer fit for pizza than the other lager monster from Italy – Peroni.

Wine

Iced Tea

NEAPOLITAN WINE

Although not famed for its wine, Campania has some ancient wineries that produce great wines. One of those is Lacryma Christi – or 'The Tears of Christ' (classic understated name) – a white based around the Falanghina grape grown in the foothills of Mount Vesuvius. It's often mentioned historically, including in Alexandre Dumas' *The Count of Monte Cristo*.

If reds are your thing, the grape to look for is Aglianico – a favourite of the Romans and the Greeks. It is used to make Taurasi – one of Campania's leading red wines.

LAMBRUSCO

Bear with us on this one. Lambrusco is a sweet, red, sparkling wine – served chilled much like prosecco. Although that sounds bonkers, it is delicious and fantastic with pizza. The tannic quality cuts through the cheese and dough a treat. Make sure you warn people before you serve it, or they might think you've lost it.

WINE & PIZZA PAIRING

Margherita: Go for a red wine with acidity and lots of fruit – maybe Barbera d'Asti, Frappato or Beaujolais Cru. Lighter reds like Gamay are also a good bet. If you go for wines that are too heavy the tannins can clash with the tomato, leaving a metallic taste in the mouth.

Pepperoni/meat: Spicy meats can probably take a wine with a little more punch: Syrah or Nero D'Avola from Sicily will work well.

White Pizza: With no tomato sauce, turn to white wine. Good options here are Soave, Pinot Grigio or Verdicchio.

OUR HOUSE SHAKEN ICED TEAS

Every kid growing up in Italy loves Estathé, the little plastic cups of iced tea with the film lid and the straw you have to stab through the top. We wanted a couple of iced teas on our menu, to give our Italian customers that nostalgic hit. Our two favourites are Earl Grey & elderflower, and builders' tea & peach. The options are limitless though, so go nuts!

1 tea bag of your choice

125ml (½ cup) boiling water

375ml (1½ cups) cold water

50ml (3 tbsp) cordial of choice

30ml (2 tbsp) lemon juice

slice of lemon, to garnish

Steep the teabag in the boiling water for two minutes. Remove the tea bag and top up with the cold water. Add the cordial and lemon juice. Fill a cocktail shaker with ice and pour in the tea mix. Shake the hell out of it and serve over ice with a slice of lemon.

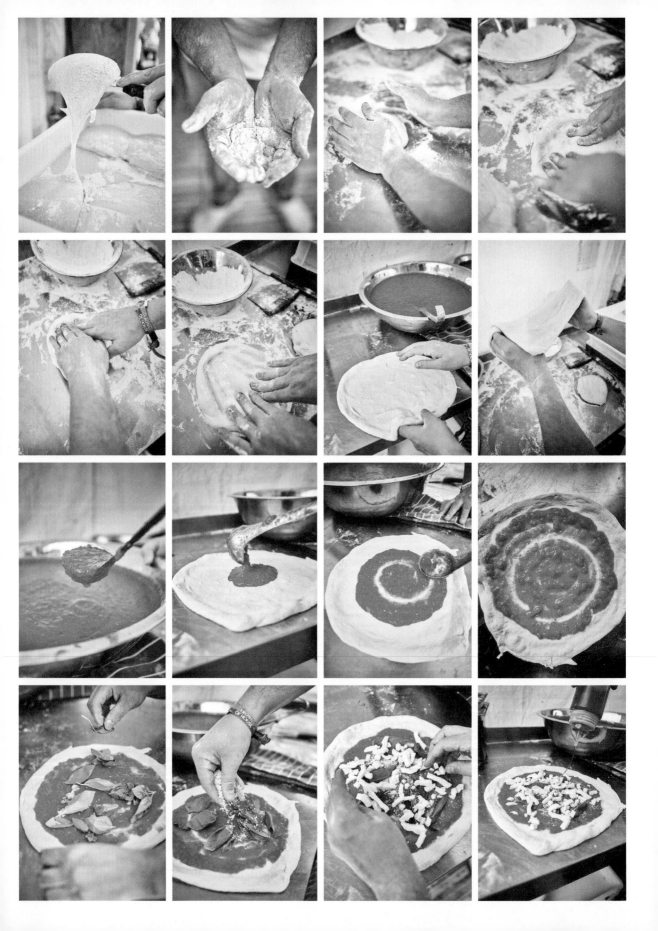

Liz Williams

Liz Williams is MD of Papa Johns in 25 different countries. She knows a thing or two about pizza...

Thom+James: What does pizza mean to Papa John's?

Liz: Pizza is at the heart of everything we do. We don't try and strive to be anything we are not; we are American pizza, pure and simple.

Thom+James: Tell us how the business functions in the UK?

Liz: Every single one of our 450 stores in the UK is run by franchisees – none are corporately owned. The dough is made fresh centrally, never frozen, and delivered to stores twice a week. The store teams refrigerate it and then bring it up to temperature on a daily basis as they use it. It's a very focused and intense process. All the pizzas are stretched to order by hand and that is a skilled process. I don't think a lot of people realise that about us!

Thom+James: You guys are about 'Better Ingredients. Better Pizza.' Right?

Liz: Exactly. And we genuinely believe that we beat our closest rivals in taste. Our tomatoes go from vine to can in under six hours, our cheese is produced in Anglesey and all our vegetables are freshly sliced in store each day.

Thom+James: So, what's the most popular Papa John pizza in the UK?

Liz: 'All The Meats' – five meats to be precise!

Thom+James: And why do you guys think pizza is so popular the world over?

Liz: I think it is a lot of things. Versatility is key – pizza is less like a type of food and more like a cuisine. It crosses religions, allergy requirements and countries – it just ticks every box!

Pizza Equations

It must be true, it's maths.

Pizza and maths have, in the past, rarely found joint airtime. But actually, listening hard in your maths classes at school might have informed your pizza eating for the rest of your life. What is also clear is that some of the top mathematical minds have been using pizza for many years to give their high-level research some healthy PR value!

The first thing to observe, which is almost proof that a higher power exists, is the formula for working out the exact size of the pizza in front of you. If you take a circular pizza with generic depth 'a' and generic radius 'z' (the distance from the centre to the edge) then the actual equation to work out the amount of pizza you have is:

$$Pi\ (\pi) \times z \times z \times a$$

Which is just too glorious, no? But who cares, we hear (some of) you ask. Well, using this formula you can actually prove some interesting stuff. For example, you wouldn't think so, but an 18-inch pizza is actually bigger than two entire 12-inch pizzas. So, think about that next time you go for a large or a medium...

Finally, Joel Haddley and Stephen Worsley from the University of Liverpool have worked out that the most scientifically accurate way to cut pizza fairly into 12 slices is the distinctly un-fun sounding 'monohedral disc tiling' method. Shown opposite, these cuts will produce scientifically perfect, equal slices. There's just one glaring omission: half the slices will be almost entirely crust! Dough!

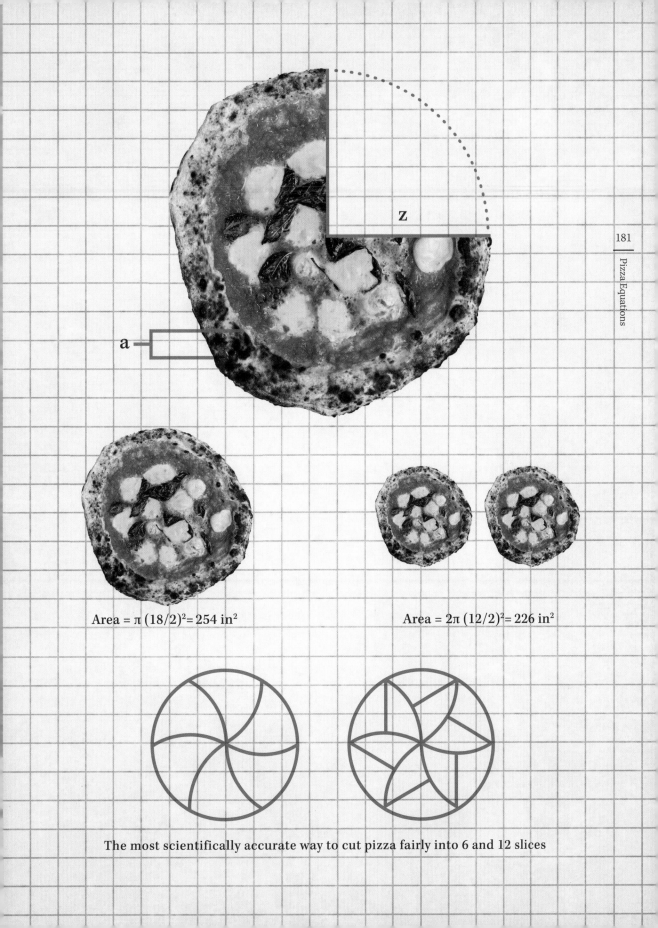

z

a

Area = π (18/2)² = 254 in²

Area = 2π (12/2)² = 226 in²

The most scientifically accurate way to cut pizza fairly into 6 and 12 slices

PIZZA PILGRIMS CITY GUIDE

PARIS

Once you've gone beyond the white tablecloths, you'll discover Paris has a great pizza scene.

It's not all croissants and galettes over in France, you know. If you're willing to take a break from traipsing around Montmartre and climbing up the Eiffel Tower, you might be pleasantly surprised at the delicious pizza offerings that Paris has to offer. Come on, ditch the touristy stuff and just go stuff your face with pizza...

DA GRAZIELLA

Quite often regarded as one of the top pizzerias in Paris, this chic little bolt hole offers some of the best Neapolitan pizzas outside of Italy, including some slightly obscure topping combinations that you'd be hard pressed to find on a pizza in Naples (the Carbonarammare – guanciale from the black pigs of Caserta, leeks, egg, black pepper and katsuobushi – we're looking at you!). The quality of the pizza is befitting for the snazzy, black, marble tables, and they have a fabulous selection of Italian wines (usually a big ask for a restaurant in Paris) to wash it all down with. Oh, and don't forget to try the Zuccona, made with fried dough and topped with pumpkin, ricotta, Gorgonzola and crispy sage. It's to die for (in more ways than one – have too many of these and your heart might give out!).

DEL POPOLO (FOOD TRUCK BY FRANCESCO SAGLIANO)

This super-cute blue pizza truck, fitted with a beautiful oven, serves fantastic Neapolitan pizza for three nights a week in the 13th and 17th arrondissements. Being a truck, the offerings are simple but, as is the case with pizza, simple is often best. This truck has a special place in our heart, due to our own humble street food origins, and you really can't go wrong whatever you order from the menu, we promise you that.

GUILLAUME GRASSO

A pizzeria that can genuinely trace its routes straight back to Pizzeria Gorizia (one of the original pizzerias in Naples from 1916), Guillaume, the grandson of one of the original Neapolitan pizzaioli, is serving up the real deal on the streets of Paris. The place is fully invested in tradition, with AVPN approval dripping from every pore, and a full menu of classic pizzas at a good price. However, there's also a good selection of more adventurous pizza options – the Corbarina was the first pizza we tried topped with balsamic vinegar. This is definitely one for the traditionalists, but that's not to be sniffed at!

PIZZERIA POPOLARE FROM BIG MAMMA GROUP

Come for the surroundings, stay for the pizza! But… be prepared to queue. Pizza Popolare is one of the most popular restaurants in Paris (the clue is in the name) and people come from all over the country for a taste of their pizza. Once inside, you're greeted by a truly stunning interior (it's hard to describe, but imagine something between *The BFG* and *Harry Potter*), an almost never-ending space filled with beautiful people having a great time! The pizza, although really delicious, always takes second place to the atmosphere of the place. Definitely one not to be missed.

BIJOU

We were taken here as a treat by the wonderful people at Laurent Perrier, and can confirm that Gennaro Nasti (not the Disney bad guy that his name suggests) is doing some of the most interesting things with pizza outside of the revered kitchens of Franco Pepe. Celebrating the new wave of 'pizza contemporaine', this pizza puts the crust first and really makes the toppings feel like they came late to the party. The bedogni, for example, really is simplicity itself, with just stracciatella, Parma ham and olive oil complementing the exemplary crust (no pizza sauce here). The pizzeria itself is tiny but perfectly formed (as the name Bijou, which means 'jewel', implies) – definitely one for hipsters or first daters.

DALMATA

Now, these guys are really crazy about pizza. Dalmata has two founders who care more about pizza than maybe anyone we have ever met. Dalmata means 'Dalmatian' in French – the pizzeria so named because of the famous leopardine spots that appear on the crust of a good Neapolitan pizza. However, they have seriously taken their namesake to the limit, only serving 101 pizzas per day… which they say is to ensure that quality remains as high as it can possibly be. Putting the pizza ahead of profits is clearly working for these guys, though, who are making some of the most exciting pizzas in Paris in the canotto style. Just make sure you get there early…

Pizza Box Art

For all those pizza Picassos out there.

In early 2015, we had a big dilemma on our hands – we wanted to change the design on our pizza box, but we couldn't agree on what it should be. And then it struck us – let's let our customers decide! And so, pizza box art was born. Since then we have had thousands and thousands of individual pieces of artwork from our customers, which now adorn the walls of our pizzas. The best attempts win a free pizza, but it's not a competition! It's just a fun way for people to express themselves and elevate the humble pizza box above its station!

Check out our online gallery at **pizzapilgrims.co.uk.**

PİZZA PİLGRİMS CİTY GUİDE

LONDON

Great pizza is relatively new here, but this is the list of our favourite pizzerias from our neck of the woods!

Since we started in the London pizza game in 2012, there has been an explosion of great pizza in the city. It wasn't that long ago that Pizza Express was leading the way and, although they'll always have a place in our hearts, we're happy to now have an amazing array of pizza joints in our local city.

SANTA MARİA

Santa Maria was started by Pasquale and Angelo, two friends from Naples who, back in 2010, blew up the UK pizza scene by serving up only the strictest execution of 'verace pizza Napoletana'. It was the first time that a lot of Londoners had tried traditional Neapolitan pizza and there was LOADS of noise about it! Serving up all the classics from the perfect Margherita to salsiccia e friarielli, the pizzas were (and still are) the closest we've tried to the true Neapolitan pizza outside of Naples. The guys also serve up some classic Neapolitan surliness alongside their pizzas, and shot to fame after the *Evening Standard* published a story about a woman who was kicked out of their pizzeria for ordering salad: 'Everyone must eat pizza', Pasquale was famously quoted. Try the bufala pizza – it's a masterpiece.

VOODOO RAY'S

This is London's best-known NYC slice joint. Named after the song by Gerald Simpson (which basically kicked off the electronic music scene in the UK), Voodoo Ray's is run by DJ Dan Beaumont, who had more experience with 12" records than 12" pizzas when he started out on the pizza scene. He headed to New York to meet up with our pal Scott Wiener (see page 204) to research what makes a great NYC pizza joint. He took inspiration from places like Bleecker Street Pizza, South Brooklyn Pizza and Roberta's to come up with his signature pies. Interestingly, they actually use a lot of classic Neapolitan ingredients to make their pizza, so it's kind of a

New York-Italy mash-up. With massive 22" pies, the slices are huge! In our opinion, it's hard to beat the classic pepperoni, but we're yet to try the infamous 'full moon slice', which is only served after midnight. All we know is that it involves bacon!

YARD SALE

Started by three mates – Nick, Johnnie and Dan – back in 2014, these guys run what they call 'pizza shops'. The story goes that they were miserable in their jobs, so they built a pizza oven in their yard and started experimenting with doughs and toppings. From there, Yard Sale grew into a love letter to pizza of ALL kinds. The shops look American, with chequered tiled floors and neon signs, but the pizza is pulled in all sorts of directions. A Neapolitan oven, NYC-style dough and toppings from all over showcase pizza that is delicious but – more importantly – fun! From the iconic Marmite and cheese pizza, to their collab with Matty Matheson to create the Brick Lane Bagel Pizza, these guys don't shy away from wacky ideas. However, they do know when to keep things simple, like when it comes to the Margherita. With their own delivery guys keeping standards high, our order of choice would be a half-and-half PSB (purple sprouting broccoli) and holy pepperoni on an 18" pizza.

HOMESLİCE

Our pals from the street food days, Homeslice was set up by three Kiwi mates who wanted to bring giant slices to the streets of London. Now they have sites across the city serving up cool and unique pizzas. The toppings are global, from bone marrow and lamb's lettuce to mushroom and sweet soy glaze. Their rule is definitely 'serve what tastes delicious' as opposed to following any rules. For us, the best order is a half-and-half of mushroom, ricotta & pumpkin seed, and courgette & artichoke, on an 18". Top tip: slather their chilli oil on everything.

SUD İTALİA

Silvestro used to work for us at Pizza Pilgrims, and we could tell then that he was itching to set up his own place. That place ended up being a Napoli blue Citroen H van that parks up in Spitalfields market serving light, fluffy Neapolitan classics to hipsters and office workers alike. These guys have a hardcore Italian following in London and may have even stolen Santa Maria's crown as the most authentic Neapolitan pizza in town. It's the quality of the ingredients that really wows us – the mozzarella is some of the best we have tried.

PİCKY WOPS

These two guys are amazing. Just their name alone is a talking point. The word 'wop' is a derogatory slur for southern Italians that is not to be used in polite company. The 'picky' bit refers to the vegan and 'healthy' bent of their menu. They do lots of different doughs, including spirulina, burned wheat, and turmeric, all offering some sort of health benefit. They also make their own vegan mozzarella and have a range of seitan and jackfruit 'meats'. The best thing to order here is the jackfruit pepperoni – a real crowd pleaser (and does not, in any way, feel healthy!).

Angelo & Pasquale

Two teenage friends from Naples, Angelo and Pasquale, met during the Italian hip-hop scene in Naples in the 1990s. Together, they opened Santa Maria, one of the first great Neapolitan pizzerias in London. The rest, as they say, is history...

Thom+James: So, why did you guys come to London in the first place?

Pasquale: I was chasing a woman of course! She was a Neapolitan but had grown up in London, so when she moved back in 2000 I knew I had to follow her.

Thom+James: Was working in pizza a tradition in your family?

Angelo: No actually! But every kid in Naples remembers going with family to a pizzeria to eat or pick up a pizza. We always watched the old guys making pizza (which they'd been doing for years) while the young guys cleaned the floors – nothing like the Naples pizza scene today.

Pasquale: The legend went that young guys couldn't touch a pizza until they'd done a decade of service in the pizzeria. You had to earn the right to be in the kitchen! Back then being a pizzaiolo was like being Maradona. Now everyone is a pizzaiolo!

Thom+James: So which do you think is the better approach?

Pasquale: I like a mix of both – experience and an element of training. It is a shame that the new generation of pizza makers do not see the old generation as something to be respected. Just like with hip-hop – the new guys do not respect the old school. To get access to the pizza oven you used to have to spend years just delivering pizzas – now things are so much easier. All we ask is that it retains a soul – pizza needs a soul! It was born in the street and it should be for everyone.

Angelo: Pizza should be about happiness! But it kind of seems to be run by social media now, which is not a good thing. I feel like the strength of the new guys on the pizza scene often lies in being good at getting attention on social media, not the actual pizza itself. People seem to worry more about Insta-likes than whether the pizza tastes good or not. All we need from pizza is for it to taste GOOD.

Thom+James: Didn't you guys famously turn someone away from Santa Maria for not ordering pizza?

Angelo: Yup. That happened. These people wanted to just buy a salad and I said if they didn't buy a pizza they had to leave. They said they would buy two bottles of wine, that we would make more money that way. I told them, no. It was out of respect for the people queuing for pizza. I would rather you have a glass of tap water and a pizza, than not order

a pizza! So they had to go. They got very upset... One of them turned out to be connected to a journalist, so the story ended up in the *Evening Standard* – with the intention of destroying our business – but unfortunately for them it actually made the restaurant MORE popular.

Pasquale: We have a simple mantra. If you have never had a Neapolitan pizza before, please try ours. If you like it, great! If you don't, don't pay. It's that simple. The breakthrough moment for us came when *Timeout* named us the best pizzeria in London in their first, and only, London pizza issue. That was two months after we opened – and our world hasn't been the same since.

Thom+James: You were a massive inspiration for us when we started our pizza journey. Why do you think the world loves pizza so much?

Pasquale: That's simple: it's fast and it just tastes so good. Not one day goes by that I don't fancy eating pizza! You've just got to remember – less is more. Pizza is all about the Margherita or Marinara. Simplicity is everything.

Angelo: We have been having pizza before we were born. Our mums were eating pizza while we were in the womb! It's in our blood.

Pasquale: Yeah I think we should feel proud that Naples created something with such global influence. Pizza is probably the most widely available food ever!

Thom+James: Exactly – whatever happens to pizza, Naples will always be the originator, and you guys will be celebrating that. That said, would you ever be tempted to put pineapple on pizza...?

Angelo: Ha, no – not yet!

Hot-Shot Chef & Collaboration Pizzas

The great thing about pizza, as they say, is that it's an edible canvas. We love teaming up with the amazing chefs, suppliers and brands that we have in London, the UK and beyond, to create some really special pizzas that you might not see in the most 'trad' spot in Naples. Here's a selection of some collaborations we've done over the years.

THE BACON & EGG NAAN PİZZA

We teamed up with the kings of Indian food, Dishoom, to create a twist on their most iconic dish – the bacon and egg naan – to support the Magic Breakfast charity who offer free breakfasts to underprivileged kids in central London. A cream cheese base, oven-roast, thick-cut bacon, mozzarella, an egg, their signature chilli ketchup, topped with coriander and green chillies. Needless to say, it was a hit.

THE FONDUTA

Inspired by the Georgian dish khachapuri, we teamed up with The Cheese Bar in London to create the ultimate cheese pizza. They supplied us with a beautiful Cornish Gouda and a Cotswold Hard cheese to blend with our Italian mozzarella and ricotta. The cheeses are melted down in our oven with a splash of white wine and garlic, then topped with a slice of prosciutto, a balsamic pickled onion and cornichons. Let the Gouda times roll!

THE PHO-ZZA

The pho stars of London, we wanted to celebrate Pho's amazing beef shin pho soup noodles (our go-to hangover cure) in pizza form. Enter: the Pho-zza! We blended their house-made spicy shrimp paste with our tomato sauce, then topped this with mozzarella, slow-cooked beef shin, crispy onions, spring onions, coriander, and served it with a wedge of lime and a little pot of Sriracha on the side for dipping. We know it sounds like it could have been a car crash, but the San Marzano tomato and chilli shrimp paste mash-up was a knockout!

THE BREAKFAST PİZZA

One of London's most prolific bloggers/critics/food people Clerkenwell Boy teamed up with us with the sole aim of creating the perfect breakfast pizza. We started with a base of house-made 'posh baked beans' using our tomato sauce and fresh cannellini beans as the base, topped this with Neapolitan fennel-seed sausage, oven-roast mushrooms and thick-cut pancetta, and then popped an egg on top. It was all washed down with an espresso negroni (which essentially involves pouring an espresso into a negroni – freaking amazing!).

THE FANCY PİZZA

The good people form Laurent Perrier called us out of the blue and asked if we fancied creating a pizza to pair with their rosé Champagne; oh, and would we like to visit the cellars in Champagne to get inspired?! So, after we got back from the vineyards we got to work on this glamour pizza. We started with a mascarpone base and then topped this with organic Scottish smoked salmon, mozzarella and Parmesan. We then sprinkled over cracked black pepper, chopped chives and served it with a wedge of lemon. The cooked smoked salmon was amazing and crisped at the side like bacon.

THE HERİTAGE TOMATO PİZZA

Italy is pretty well known for tomatoes but, in the UK on the Isle of Wight, there is a microclimate that allows the sweetest, most beautiful tomatoes to grow. We wanted to show them off on a pizza in the purest way possible, so we baked a simple white pizza with buffalo mozzarella, garlic, Parmesan and basil and served it with a salad of the tomatoes in all shapes and sizes, simply dressed in olive oil and salt. It was on the menu for summer and one of our best-selling pizzas.

THE LAHAM BAGİNE PİZZA

Cook for Syria is an incredible charity that helps the refugee crisis in Syria. They asked us to develop a pizza that celebrated Syrian food and culture. After a trip down Edgware Road in London, we came across a traditional Syrian flatbread called laham bagine – a pizza-style bread topped with spiced lamb mince and za'atar. We added an Italian twist using our dough, mozzarella, a slow-cooked lamb ragu packed with Syrian spices, and topped it off with a little cinnamon, cumin, coriander, za'atar and sesame seeds. A real highlight for us was when a Syrian customer tried the pizza and said it reminded him of happy days at home.

THE MEAT FEAST

A lot of people love a meat-feast pizza, but not everyone admits it. We wanted to create our own twist on this as an ode to the classic meat feast you get from late-night pizza shops. Cannon & Cannon teamed up with us to offer their amazing range of British cured meats. We tasted every product they had to offer and landed on four meats to star on this pizza, from the four corners of the UK. The hams were too good to cook so we baked a white pizza, sliced it into quarters and then dressed each slice with a different meat. By complete accident, we managed to create the ULTIMATE accompaniment to beer. Take us back!

THE PİZZA BURGER

One of our favourite burger joints in London, we teamed up with Bleecker's owner Zan to create a pizza burger. This was made up of fresh basil pesto, yellow datterini tomatoes, smoked pancetta, a Bleecker double patty and topped off with a mini burrata. The pizza burger... where two perfect foods meet!

THE HAWAİİ NOT

Just after Brexit happened in the UK, we decided that a more important referendum was needed: should pineapple be on pizza? Together with Neil Rankin (of Temper), we set about reinventing the Hawaiian pizza. We roasted pineapples whole in our pizza oven, then marinated them in honey, lime and chilli. We paired the pineapple with spicy 'nduja sausage and jalapeños to create a sweet, savoury, smoky, spicy pizza that we named the 'Hawaii Not'. Every pizza was accompanied with a voting slip. We had over 10,000 votes and the Hawaii Not was voted a success, but only by 256 votes! We discovered that PINEAPPLE DOES BELONG ON PIZZA!

THE BİSCOFF BROWNİE S'MORE PİZZA

For our 7th birthday we teamed up with the one-and-only Cupcake Jemma (owner and creative cake force behind Crumbs & Doilies bakery). She helped us come up with a sweet pizza (or sweetza) to rival the Nutella Ring (see page 164). We started with a mascarpone base, crumbled over Jemma's signature brownies, then scattered over crushed Biscoff biscuits and some mini marshmallows. After coming out of the oven, it was served with a ball of vanilla ice cream, Biscoff cream and more marshmallows. Not one for the faint-hearted... but the combo of hot salty pizza dough topped with all that sugary goodness and cold ice cream was a match made in heaven.

Jens Hofma

We had a chat with Jens Hofma,
the CEO of Pizza Hut Restaurants UK.
How's the view from the top Jens?

Thom+James: So, like us, Pizza Hut has 'pizza'
in its name (something that we attribute to most
of our success!). Is pizza at the heart of what
Pizza Hut is about?

Jens: Yup, completely. I don't think we will ever
be known for anything as much as we are for
great-tasting pizza. Whenever we try to broaden
that, and attempt to do some other great stuff
as well, it never really punches through. We are
definitely a pizza place.

Thom+James: When we think of Pizza Hut –
and we think most people feel the same – we
think of deep pan pizza. It's quite a unique offer
in the UK and no one really does deep pan like
you. You are proud of that pizza legacy, right?

Jens: To me it demonstrates how versatile
pizza really is – there is an infinity of different
executions. I think for many years Pizza Hut
was led astray; we saw the rapid growth of
more 'authentic' Italian chains and we started
to think about our own pizza offering. Perhaps
our pizza might need to be more Italian? More
authentic? Have a thinner crust? I did a pizza
safari in Soho, before Pizza Pilgrims existed,
and I went to a very artisanal, family-run pizza
restaurant. I had a bit of a chat with the owner
and he asked where I worked. For a moment,
I wondered whether I should tell him or not,
but did then reveal I worked for Pizza Hut. His
immediate response was 'I absolutely love Pizza

Hut, I go there once a month and have your deep pan pizza. It's the one thing you just can't get anywhere else!'. From then on, I realised that we should be celebrating what we are, not trying to be what we are not. People should embrace the huge variety of pizza we have all around the world.

Thom+James: You're 100% right. Especially when you have created something so iconic that has been around for so many years – how can you mess with it!?

Jens: Exactly. There is actually a lot of craft that goes into the product. Our kitchens are quite large, as the actual proving and retarding of the dough is done in store. The rising of the dough has to happen there and then, and has to be treated with care so it doesn't collapse. There is a lot of operational complexity around creating a great deep pan pizza, so we should be proud of it. We are an American interpretation of pizza – we are not trying to be an Italian pizza.

Thom+James: So, is deep pan your top seller?

Jens: Thin crust is about 25% of our sales, and 35% deep pan. The rest is stuffed crust and cheesy bites, which we would never want to move away from.

Thom+James: We love a stuffed crust – its ingenious and fun! You guys invented it in 1995, and within a year it was one of your most popular products. And there is even an ad with Donald Trump. Genius.

Jens: There was also an ad with Gorbachev. And a Gareth Southgate ad! We don't really do massive TV advertising campaigns any more – I prefer to invest in the restaurant food and decor – but I think that our presence on social media gives us the opportunity to be a little cheeky every now and again.

Thom+James: So, can we talk about the buffet for a bit – it's such an iconic part of Pizza Hut.

Jens: It has great advantages: instant access

to food, very generous, great variety. I like the freedom that the buffet brings to our restaurants; it makes the vibe easy going.

Thom+James: Can we ask about Pizza Hut's propensity to develop slightly outlandish pizzas? The Crown Crust for example…

Jens: We actually created the Crown Crust in the UK for the Diamond Jubilee! We even did a video of the Royal Family coming to Pizza Hut! Our wacky ideas come from all over the world: we've done a macaroni cheese pizza (that was good!), a cheeseburger pizza, hot dog pizza… We do them to create a bit of a shockwave, but it is important to me that they're all still executed in a quality way.

Thom+James: Why do you think that pizza is so globally adored? Why is it always the food people turn to when going through a breakup?!

Jens: I think it is just the ultimate comfort food. It's a lot of carbs, it's bread, it's warm cheese. It's gooey. Its very tactile – you can eat it with you hands and therefore instantly create a very intimate relationship with what you're eating. That doesn't always happen when using a knife and fork. And, most importantly, its round.

Thom+James: You think that the fact it is round is a factor?

Jens: Absolutely. Round is inclusive. Round says sharing – look what it says on the wall ['The Hut is made for sharing!']. Pizza is a fuss-free and easily accessible communal experience.

Thom+James: OK, last question. Have Pizza Hut ever created a pizza that was too outlandish for the mainstream market?

Jens: Well, a few of my colleagues are lobbying for a marijuana pizza! Apparently, it tastes fabulous. But that won't be appearing on our menus at the moment – even with some of the states now legalising use. We also did a Marmite stuffed crust a few years ago. Now *that* was a controversial one!

Eating Pizza

How do you eat yours?

Walking through our pizzeria we see it all. People from every walk of life eating pizza in every imaginable way. How you eat your slice is the true inkblot test of the pizza world. On the next few pages, we've outlined eight pizza-eating techniques we see people using and asked the UK's leading body language specialist, Adrianne Carter (AKA 'The Face Whisperer'), to give us an insight into what pizza-eating styles reveal about the type of person you are. So, get ready to understand yourself a little better...

THE NEAPOLITAN HANDS-FREE

Poor old Bill De Blasio, the New York Mayor, was given no end of stick for eating his pizza with a knife and fork. The truth is, the OG pizza eaters in Naples always eat with a knife and fork. The reasoning goes that pizza is too important to rush, and you should sit down, relax with a good glass of wine and take the time to enjoy your pizza (with a knife and fork!).

The Face Whisperer: This person will be conscious of not making a mess and keeping their hands and face as clean as possible. They are probably the tidiest person in the house and office and like to do things properly and in a set way.

THE CIGAR

We see this a lot in our pizzerias, and the people that do it always look in-the-know. The main benefit here is supposed to be that, in every mouthful, you get a bit of everything, from crust to sauce to cheese. You roll the slice from the tip to the crust to create a 'cigar', then eat it from top to bottom. The jury's out on this one for us. Surely you want to celebrate every part of the pizza separately?!

The Face Whisperer: The term 'party pooper' definitely springs to mind. This pizza eater sounds like the person who takes all the fun and enjoyment out of a party. They're also likely to be constantly in a rush, having to absorb a lot of info at once.

THE BLOTTER

We love that scene in *Along Came Polly* when Philip Seymour Hoffman coaches Ben Stiller on pizza grease after Stiller's character blots his slice with napkins to reduce the oil. There are two problems with the blot: 1. Hoffman's character is right, the grease has all the flavour; 2. The napkins you get at a NY slice joint are about as absorbent as clingfilm (plastic wrap). If you have to take some of the oil off, the only technique is to hold the slice up in the air and squeeze it like you're milking a cow (but this makes you look like a weirdo, so we wouldn't advise it!).

The Face Whisperer: This person is scared to enjoy themselves and is likely to worry about all sorts of things. It's time to stop worrying and eat the pizza, oil and all!

THE NEAPOLITAN PIZZA BOAT

So, you know what we said about Neapolitans using knives and forks to eat pizza? Well, there are exceptions... In Naples, pizza is a meal you can eat any time of the day: breakfast, lunch or dinner. So, if you don't have time to sit down and have to grab a slice on the go, there's only one way to eat sloppy Naples pizza without getting cheese and tomato all over you: the pizza boat. You fold the slice in half, then tuck the end over, creating a vessel for the cheese and sauce that ensures no leakage. True pro stuff.

The Face Whisperer: A person who wants to ensure they don't miss a bit of the good stuff or make a mess. Probably Mr or Mrs Practical in their daily life, and the person we all turn to for a practical solution to our everyday problems.

THE SNAG AND DRAG

In our pizza lives, we have only ever seen this once, and we can still see the guy who did it, clear as day, sitting in our pizzeria. An older man of about 60 came in, ordered a Margherita and, when it arrived, picked up the plate, grabbed the pizza with his teeth, pulled it towards him and began to work his way through it straight off the plate. It was much like watching a snake eat a baby deer, and we respect him for that...

The Face Whisperer: This person does not care what other people think of how they behave or what they do. Possibly has no friends to monitor their behaviour.

THE REVERSE SHUFFLE

Crusts first. We don't know about you, but we just don't trust this method. Based on what we see in our pizzerias, we think about 1 in 20 people prefer to eat on the dark side. Our theory is this: these people are those who like the crust the least, and therefore want to get it over with as soon as possible. The main issue here is that you lose the handle god gave pizza and end up with sauce all over your hands. Hmmm…

The Face Whisperer: This is the rebellious pizza eater. The one who wants to do things differently and not follow the crowd – even when it's impractical to do so.

CRUST LEAVER

There's only one thing worse than eating the crusts first… not eating them at all! We feel this must be a hangover from when you were a kid and your mum would tell you to eat the crusts of your sandwich. Some people are really down on the crust of a pizza but, the truth is, if it's a good pizza the crust is the best bit! Also, by not eating the crusts you're wasting almost half the pizza! Poor form in our book…

The Face Whisperer: This suggests the kind of person who can never be bothered to finish a task, and often ducks out at the last minute. There are probably a lot of DIY projects in their house that get started but never finished!

THE TONY MANERO

Depending on when you were born, this technique can also be referred to as 'The Joey Special' (from *Friends*). In 1978 John Travolta put Brooklyn pizza on the big screen when he played the role of Tony Manero in *Saturday Night Fever* – the paint-slinging disco fiend with a penchant for good pizza. His special move? Stacking one slice on top of the other and eating both in one go. Combine this with a flare-fuelled strut and you have one of the most iconic pizza scenes in movie history.

The Face Whisperer: Double enjoyment! One flavour or two? In going for the same flavour on both slices, this person knows what they like in life and aren't afraid to enjoy it! Different topping combos on each slice reveal a person who isn't afraid to mix things up and is always looking to max out their enjoyment. They also possibly suffer from FOMO…

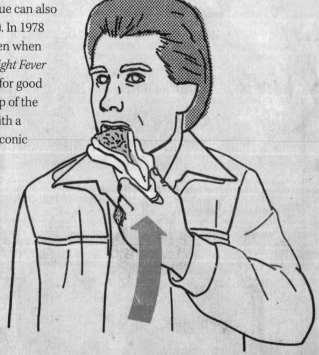

James doing the Tony Manero at Lombardi's, Manhattan.

Pizza hybrids

The kind of hybrid that is definitely not saving the planet.

PIZZA HUT CROWN CRUST CARNIVAL

This is it, the king of all pizza hybrids; it's even called the Crown Crust. Pizza Hut in the Middle East have some serious form in the pizza hybrid market, but we think this is the one that pushed it over the edge. Even Jay Rayner, famed UK restaurant critic, deemed this one worth trying (only once by the sounds of it). This cheeseburger pizza mash-up marks the coming together of probably the two most loved fast food groups in the world, but it's clear that this pairing wasn't made to last, perhaps other than in your imagination…

GENUINE NEAPOLITAN AMERICANA PIZZA

It is not only the global chains who are up to the hybrid game. The majority of pizzerias in Naples will proudly display on their menu the aptly named Pizza Americana. This is essentially a classic bianca Neapolitan pizza topped with sliced and fried hot dogs.

For a city that famously takes their pizza incredibly seriously, it feels a little, well, relaxed. But, to be fair, it's delicious.

STUFFED CRUST PIZZA

It says a lot about the world we live in that a pizza with a crust stuffed with cheese now almost seems like the norm. The crust is the place where American pizza and Neapolitan pizza can pretty much forever be separated. Our American friends see the crust of a pizza as the boring bit, simply a vehicle for toppings or dips, while over in Naples, people see the crust as the pizza's *raison d'être*, with the toppings merely the garnish of a quality dough.

Stuffed crust has grown and grown in popularity and is clearly here to stay. It is ground zero for a lot of the creations in this section. Its infamy is probably best highlighted by the first advert Pizza Hut made for the product, featuring a certain Donald Trump demonstrating how he now eats his pizza the 'wrong way' – crust first.

PIZZA HUT CONE CRUST

Rather like the Sex Pistols leading to a proliferation of punk bands in the seventies (many actually better than the Pistols but always without the visceral hit of the new), so the Cone Crust appeared out of the shadow cast by the aforementioned Crown Crust. The Cone Crust actually has many more fans in the taste department, and its innovation is really more an evolution than revolution. Still, we're not really sure how Pizza Hut can back up the claim: 'Fun Starts with a Cone' ... what?!

HOT DOG STUFFED CRUST PIZZA & HOT DOG CRUST

An inevitable development of the stuffed crust, this is, in many ways, the high point of the pizza hybrid. The bottom line is – it just works. The reviews are positive and, other than the calorie count, it is seen as a triumph in pizza creation. The original hot dog stuffed crust actually debuted in the UK – quite a rarity – and soon spread across the world. This led to the Pizza Hut creation of a crust of individual hot dogs, taking the idea to its logical conclusion. Hats off to them.

DOMINO'S DOUBLE DECADENCE

The Domino's Double Decadence was a genius creation – two pizza bases sandwiching a layer of garlic and herb cream cheese and then topped with your usual pizza topping choice.

The really shocking thing about this is that it has been discontinued by Domino's – to the general outrage of the online community: 'This pizza changed my life and since it has been taken away it has left a hole. I don't order pizza anymore because of it.' There is even an online petition campaigning to bring it back!

POUTINE PIZZA

Poutine is a particularly decadent dish – a Canadian delicacy of fries topped with cheese curds and gravy – perfect for keeping you warm through even the coldest Canadian winter. Adding it to a pizza just seems to make sense, and actually makes it a little easier to eat. Winning.

PIZZA HUT PIZZA FRAGRANCE

Not the hybrid you were probably expecting when you started reading this section, Pizza Hut in Canada have actually created a limited-edition fragrance that smells of freshly made pizza dough. They only made around 100 bottles though, so they were either not really 100% into the idea or were scared that its power should not be spread too widely.

PIZZA CONES

Pizza cones take the ingredients of pizza and convert them into the form of an ice cream cone, meaning the whole edifice is completely edible. It is rather like a game of 'flavour of, form of' has got out of hand.

While the convenience is hard to deny – which may explain their proliferation across the world (including some big advocates in Italy itself!) – we just can't understand how you could possibly eat one without getting third-degree burns.

PIZZA CAKE

This hybrid creation does not appear to be available commercially – which is rather telling in itself – although the home baking maestros at Pillsbury do have the recipe on their website. Essentially four pizzas stacked on top of each other, it is, in many ways, a masterpiece. In another way, it definitely isn't.

Scott Wiener

Scott Wiener is the legend who runs pizza tours of NYC – yes, that is a real job!

Thom+James: So, big first question, which is your second favourite pizza city after New York?

Scott: Hmm. I like Portland a lot, and San Francisco is pretty good too. Portland pizza has loads of variety and people there have recently taken on learning pizza from the ground up, making bad-ass pizzas with no foot in pizza history at all!

Thom+James: Tell us when your love affair with pizza began?

Scott: Well, when you live around here, you eat pizza at least twice a week. And you don't go out for pizza, you pick it up and bring it home. It was the one thing that the family loved doing together. I just fell in love with the ritual of it all, the smell of the box and the fact that it's the only food that satisfies everyone.

Thom+James: So, how did you get into pizza tours?

Scott: Having grown up in Jersey, it wasn't until after college that I started to realise the significance of NYC pizza. I ended up quitting my job and gave myself 6 months to figure out what I wanted to do with my life. Spending those months hanging out in pizzerias eventually just transitioned into pizza tours!

Thom+James: Amazing. We've always thought that you use pizza as a lens to view the whole world.

Scott: Exactly – it is not just about the food. It's about the community, too.

Thom+James: So, the big claim to fame – you have more pizza boxes than anyone else in the world?

Scott: Yup. And I have a Guinness World Record to show for it! I don't think I cared about pizza boxes at all until the moment I became obsessed with them. When I was growing up, all the pizza boxes were the same. They were white cardboard boxes with smudgy red printing. Nothing special. So you can imagine my surprise when I noticed yellow pizza boxes on a trip to Israel. It blew my mind. From then on, I always noticed the pizza box. It became more than just a vessel for transporting the best food in the world, it was a piece of cultural significance. It's funny how the things we always take for granted are the most interesting once you put them under a microscope. A pizza box carried horizontally is just a pizza box, but viewed vertically it's a piece of art.

Thom+James: Are there any pizza box innovations that you've seen that you think should be adopted by others?

Scott: Yes, but they tend to be too expensive. There are boxes that breathe! Boxes that absorb moisture! I can't see the standard pizza box changing though. I just hope the sustainability of them will improve, with a move to using compressed fibre instead of cardboard.

Thom+James: What about a reusable box?

Scott: That won't work in New York! Do you expect customers to wash a box and return it?

Thom+James: Very true! So, talk to us about Slice Out Hunger.

Scott: It's a non-profit that fundraises for hunger relief organisations around the US through pizza-driven events and campaigns. Some restaurants have a speciality pizza on the menu and proceeds from each sale go to SOH.

We have one big event each year, 'Dollar Slice Night'. Our plan is to expand our $1 Pizza Parties to college campuses across America.

Thom+James: Amazing stuff! On that note, is it still possible to get dollar slices in New York?!

Scott: Only if you are drunk enough! If you're not drunk it will taste crappy.

Thom+James: OK, well when was the last time you could get a decent dollar slice in NYC?

Scott: 1986!

Thom+James: Classic. Next question – what's the strangest pizza you've ever eaten?

Scott: I had a 24 karat gold pizza once. Now *that* was bonkers. It had a squid ink dough base, and was topped with truffle, foie gras, caviar and literal GOLD. It was disgusting. And it was $2,700! Luckily I didn't have to pay because it was for a TV show...

Thom+James: Here's a big question. Why is pizza so important to humans? Why is it a food that people rely on?

Scott: It's the most democratic of all foods. Everyone can afford it, it's portable, it adjusts itself to your needs, and you can top it with anything you want to make you happy. It's non-exclusive. Which makes it a universal language. We can make a pizza for people with allergies. No gluten? No worries. Pizza will never fail you.

Thom+James: It's as big as religion for some people!

Scott: But when you disagree on religion there's often frustration involved. When you disagree about pizza it's usually more a conversation of mutual respect!

Thom+James: How many pizzerias are there in New York now?

Scott: Almost 2,000... it's a lot!

Thom+James: And finally, if pizza is the most iconic food of New York, what's in second place?

Scott: Hmm... It's probably got to be the bagel!

'I don't think I cared about pizza boxes at all until the moment I became obsessed with them. When I was growing up, all the pizza boxes were the same. They were white cardboard boxes with smudgy red printing. Nothing special. So you can imagine my surprise when I noticed yellow pizza boxes on a trip to Israel. It blew my mind. From then on, I always noticed the pizza box. It became more than just a vessel for transporting the best food in the world, it was a piece of cultural significance. It's funny how the things we always take for granted are the most interesting once you put them under a microscope. A pizza box carried horizontally is just a pizza box, but viewed vertically it's a piece of art.'

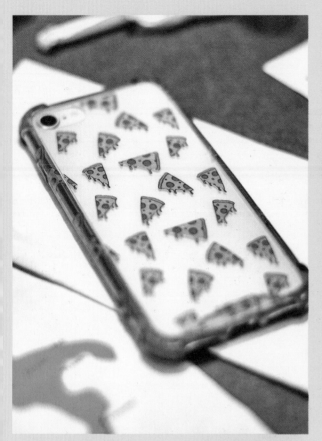

Pizza Facts

An assortment of random bits of crust we have picked up:

- **The pepperoni pizza emoji is the most used emoji in the US.**

- The US eats around 100 acres of pizza every day.

- **Anchovies are the least favourite pizza topping in the US – pepperoni is the favourite!**

- The Hawaiian pizza was invented in, you guessed it... Canada. The president of Iceland later tried to ban it!

- **A pizza was (probably) the first thing to be ordered online – in 1974 in Michigan.**

- Chuck E. Cheese, the famous US pizza chain, was set up by the founder of Atari.

- **Bill Murray used to work in a pizza place.**

- Macaulay Culkin, star of *Home Alone*, later formed a Velvet Underground cover band that was called Pizza Underground.

- **Pizza Hut delivered a pizza to the International Space Station in 2001.**

- Saturday night is the biggest night for ordering pizza and, rather oddly, Halloween is the biggest pizza night of the year. Spooky.

- **Domino's delivery drivers cover 10 million miles per week in the US alone.**

- Pizza Hut once tried to engrave their logo on the moon with lasers.

- **The risk of oesophageal cancer is reduced significantly if pizza is consumed at least once a week.**

- The Neapolitan Margherita is a UNESCO protected food.

- **The three largest global Pizza chains are: No.1 Domino's, No.2 Pizza Hut and No. 3 Little Caesars.**

Scott Bush

Say hello to Scott Bush,
Domino's UK ops director.

Thom+James: What's the mantra at Domino's?

Scott: You need to be seeking quality all the time, not just engineering a product for profit. And the other key mantra for us is 'time is the enemy of food'. Pizza doesn't get better in the box. It has got to be quick, good value and taste really good.

Thom+James: And why do you feel pizza is so important to people all over the world?

Scott: Firstly, I think it's because pizza is the one food that is truly personal. For example, we have 18 pizzas on our menu, but with the varied topping combinations there are up to 1,000,000 possible pizzas! There is something unique for everyone – even the fussiest palate – and you don't really get that with any other take-out food. The second reason pizza is so popular, is that it is a visual product – it is big and flat and round – you know what you're getting with pizza,

from the moment you open the box, all the way through to the moment that slice lands in your mouth. The excitement builds for every mouthful. Genius. Third reason – you eat it with your hands, anywhere and any time – no need for a knife and fork. You can eat it at 3am, or for breakfast. And you can share it – you can't share a kebab.

Thom+James: And what's the number one pizza you sell in the UK?

Scott: Pepperoni Passion is number one, but Margherita is a close second.

Thom+James: OK, elephant in the room. Double Decadence. That was something genuinely unique to you guys and it was genius. Why did that go from your menu?!

Scott: Sometimes you've just got to take things away to give people a reason to return when it comes back on the menu…!

PIZZA PILGRIMS CITY GUIDE

NEW YORK

Even if they didn't invent pizza, you would think they did!

New York is, as a city, completely synonymous with pizza. We don't think there is a street in Manhattan that doesn't have a pizzeria (or 100 pizzerias) – even when you say the word pizza in your head it is with a New York accent. While pizza wasn't invented here (see our pizza history section on page 24), there is no doubt that New York has a place at the top table of pizza; a city that should not be missed on any pizza world tour (that's a thing, right?). We spent an amazing week in and around New York with the legend that is Scott Wiener (see our interview on page 204) and we ate a LOT of pizza. Here is a collection of our favourite spots. There's a multitude of reasons why these joints made the cut, but ultimately it comes down to the pies, the vibes and the history!

SCARR'S

We were blown away by this relatively low-profile slice shop serving great pizza in a cool setting. The pizza quality was excellent, but it was really the vibe that set this one apart for us. They've found a nice balance between pizzeria, dive bar and general hangout, and it was probably the closest we've come to feeling like we were eating pizza on a movie set. Also, and this is a nice touch, they sell both Coke and Pepsi, so we did our very own 'Pepsi Challenge' while we enjoyed our slices (spoiler: Coke wins).

JOE'S

For us, this is as close as you can get to the NY slice you envisage in your dreams. The original Joe's Pizza has been in the village since 1975, but there are a few dotted around elsewhere. This is a no-nonsense set up, but that's exactly what you want from it. There is plenty of debate about whether to go for the plain cheese or the fresh mozzarella but for us the former is where it's at. Add some Parmesan to your slice at the table (weirdly, it kinda feels like you are making it healthier by doing that…) and get stuck in.

The classic pepperoni nonna slice at Prince St. – check the cupping!

Oldest pizza oven in the US of A.

JOHN'S

Another institution (they claim to still be using the same coal oven that the original owner built in 1929), John's serves a mean pie in a location where history oozes from every pore. Every inch of the walls is scrawled with the names of people marking their visit and the celebrity photos are everywhere. Frank Sinatra even ate pizza here – and you can tell why. The sausage pizza is our top pick at John's and just has to be tried (note: there are no slices on offer so you will have to order the whole pie). Definitely worth the wait in line.

PAULIE GEE'S & PAULIE GEE'S SLICE SHOP

Paulie Gee is now a Greenpoint legend, having decided that, instead of retiring at the end of his career, he wanted to open a pizzeria to celebrate his love of pizza and entertain friends. The result? One of the warmest, buzziest, most inventive pizzerias New York City has to offer. The place has a unique family feel, with Paulie there almost every night greeting guests and sharing his homemade limoncello. Lacking the standard NYC badge of honour (longevity), the pizza has to do all the talking here – and it sure does. The menu is one of the most extensive and interesting we have ever seen and the Neapolitan-style pizzas literally fly out of the domed oven. So many of the offerings shouldn't work but, somehow, they just do. And some of Paulie's pizzas, such as The Hellboy, have become iconic. Alongside the original Neapolitan-inspired pizzeria in Greenpoint, Paulie has now also set up a New York slice shop. It's a super cool place – straight out the '70s interior-wise, with strip lighting and old-school Coke machines – but his playful inventiveness is there in plain sight. The sesame-based grandma slice is genius. As are the takeaway pizza boxes featuring Paulie's trademark black glasses perched on the quintessential winking chef illustration. Definitely worth a visit!

LOMBARDI'S

So, this is it. The place in America where pizza began. The only place you will find a business that has been making pizza longer than Lombardi's is in Naples – and this is not up for debate. Lombardi's so perfectly encapsulates an old-school pizzeria it's almost clichéd. It's like the kind of pizzeria you would see in a Disney movie or on an episode of The Simpsons: chequered table cloths, uniformed waiters, memorabilia gilding the walls. The pizza, if we are being honest (we always are when it comes to pizza), is not the best New York has to offer, but you can taste here, more than anywhere, the effect of that coal oven and the near century that it has been turning out pizzas. A must visit for NYC – if for the history more than the pizza.

PRINCE ST. PIZZA

Prince St. Pizza is a little hole in the wall on, you guessed it, Prince Street. You won't miss it though as it will have a long line of pizza lovers outside it at all times waiting for their fix. In this case, that fix is their world-famous square slice, most likely topped with the most perfectly cupped pepperoni you ever will see. This is a doughy but deeply satisfying pizza experience – one of our favourites in all of New York. There is little else to say, other than to make sure this one is on your list.

JJ of Scarr's.

Brothers eating their pizza in sync.

ROBERTA'S

Roberta's is definitely the cool kid on the block – basically a house party masquerading as a pizzeria. The pizzas are fantastic (Neapolitan-style) and the atmosphere is on point. For New York it is definitely a little out of the way, but it is worth the trip for sure and a great place to settle in for the evening (not least, as the bar offer is extensive).

BEST PİZZA

Frank Pinello – host of Vice's *The Pizza Show* – started this neighbourhood joint in 2010 after working at some of NYC's best pizza hot-spots. The place is a perfect little slice joint with a nice local vibe and a great selection of pies on offer by the slice. It's definitely worth the trip over to Williamsburg – you'll even be in with a chance of seeing a pizza celebrity on his home turf.

EMMY SQUARED

This place is not strictly a pizza joint, offering a range of non-pizza options on their menu, but that does not detract from the quality of pizza they do serve! Detroit-style – and handily split into 'Reds' and 'Whites' – this is great pizza with loads of interesting topping options and a delicious, doughy crust. Served as a traybake divided into 6 slices, we would suggest that at least one whole pizza per person is where you'll want to be at.

Dİ FARA

OK, so this is one of the best stories in the pizza game. Domenico De Marco came over to NYC from Caserta in Italy in 1965, decided to open a pizzeria, and Di Fara first opened its doors that same year. 'Dom' has been there ever since, hand crafting each and every pizza they make – he's 82 now! He does an amazing job and clearly puts so much love and care into every single pie that goes through his electric oven. However, there is one small issue... We made the pilgrimage out to Di Fara one lunchtime all ready to order, but we were told there was over a two hour wait for a slice. Sadly, we had to get to the airport, so we didn't get to taste the pizza (although there were enough people waiting their two hours who assured us it was worth the wait). So – as much as it pains us – we have no review for you on this one, just the promise of the pizza-lovers waiting in line!

SAM'S

Sam's is straight out of a Scorsese movie. Red chequered tablecloths, neon signs, strip lighting – it's the whole nine yards. Lovingly referred to as a 'red sauce' joint, Sam's serves up the Italian-American classics. Baked clams, meatballs, spaghetti with Marinara sauce and, of course, the pizza. Louis runs the show here with a firm grip. His dad Mario was the pizza chef here for 60 years so he knows the menu. He'll tell you what to eat, but just make sure the clams, sausage pie and a cocktail called 'The Stinger' is on that order slip.

The pizza chefs at John's on Bleecker Street.

Louis, of Sam's in Brooklyn. Showing us that famous New York hospitality.

Paulie Gee

From pizza parties at home,
to one of NY's most revered
Pizzerias. Paulie tells us it's never
too late to start your life in pizza.

Thom+James: So Paulie, we have to start with
your pizza story. How did you end up getting
into pizza so late in life?

Paulie: Well, I never really knew what I wanted
to do in life and I ended up spending my life
doing something I had no passion for. So, I
started looking for other things to do. I loved to
cook for friends and family and they kept saying
I should open my own restaurant. However, the
idea seemed daunting to me. A friend even came
along who wanted to back me in a breakfast
and lunch franchise business, but I didn't want
to follow someone else's recipes. All the while,
I just loved pizza and I realised that operating a

pizzeria was simpler than running a full service
restaurant. That realisation emboldened me, so
I built a pizza oven in my garden and used that
as a tool to get myself used to cooking pizza.
I invited people over and experimented on them
with my pizza recipes. This was in 2007 and I
was blown away by my ability to actually make
pizza in a wood burning oven. Slowly but surely
my pizza gained traction and bloggers like Adam
Kuban started to write about me. I'd always been
a pizza enthusiast, so it was great to be making
my own pizza successfully, rather than just
eating other people's. My love of pizza started
in Trenton, N.J. They have amazing tomato pies

down there. But my mind was really blown when I first tried a pizza at Totonno's (who claim to be the first pizzeria in Brooklyn). Once I saw that I was able to make pizza that others would be willing to purchase I took out some equity from my house, found a few other guys who would put in the rest of the money, and we were off! It was a total nightmare project, but we got there in the end.

Thom+James: So, you basically went from running pizza parties in your home, to having your own pizzeria? No middle ground?

Paulie: That is correct. I just found out everything I needed to know by speaking to other pizzeria owners and listening to what they told me. They were all so generous with their knowledge and encouragement, especially Mark Iacono from Lucali's, Mathieu Palombino of Motorino, Chris Parachini from Roberta's and the guys at Nomad pizza, who had the same oven as me. But I started with Peter Reinhart's *American Pie* pizza book and took it from there. Pies that I developed at home are still on my menu today… Obviously, I've been inspired by others for some of my pizza offerings, but then, so has everyone in the business. For example, I borrowed the Delboy, which evolved into the Hellboy, from Motorino, who had borrowed it from Fornino – and then you guys stole it from me!

Thom+James: How do you feel about pizzerias sharing pie ideas between them?

Paulie: I'm all good with emulating ideas. I do think they should pay homage though – it can't be stealing! For instance, I was inspired by Roberta's Speckenwolf, so I called our version the Specktacle 261 which is Roberta's address. I have actually trademarked the Hellboy, so at least you guys can't steal the name!

Thom+James:: And was the pizzeria busy from day one?

Paulie: Sort of – people were very supportive. We got a big bump once we got a liquor licence. But it really kicked off when Mathieu from Motorino got me on a Food Network show because he wasn't available. From that moment things went really crazy. I was eventually featured on *The Today Show* which made things even busier.

Thom+James: And where did the oven style come from? We love it!

Paulie: Well, I had a really ugly green oven at home, so I wanted something better. Something with an Italian feel but subtle. I saw a sun motif at the Sun Valley Ski Resort in Idaho, and I thought, that is the perfect thing to put on my oven to make it feel Mediterranean. I just added the word Napoli in cobalt blue, a couple of lemon bunches and my oven design was born. I showed pictures of my home oven to Stefano Ferrara in Naples and he created my famous oven. I was one of the first people in America to have one of his ovens!

Thom+James: Talk to us about the punny names for your pizza – they are genius! Do the names or the pies come first?

Paulie: Well, that all came from Roberta's, those guys started the pun thing. They were a great inspiration to me in general. Their place was like the *Little Rascals* had said 'let's build a pizzeria!' and made me realise that I didn't need $1M to make a great pizzeria. And they did punny names. I usually start with a music reference and take it from there, but I will never put a pie on a menu without a good name. I have actually gone with a great pie name even though the pizza sucked… A pie with spaghetti squash and lemon juice on it: Sergio Limone! Great name, awful pie! I took it off the menu very quickly.

Thom+James: And why did the slice shop come to be?

Paulie: I no longer wanted to put my wood-fired pizza in a box because it loses much of its character, but the residents of North Brooklyn were disappointed that take-out was no longer available! Realising that NY-style pizza travelled and reheated well, I decided to open up a pizzeria that paid homage to the Brooklyn slice shops of the '60s and '70s.

Thom+James: Genius. Gotta respect the pizza! Final question then, why is pizza so important to the human race?

Paulie: That's easy – because it is accessible. It's delicious and high quality, but it's still affordable. Everyone can afford to eat 'the best pizza in the world' and that is a rare thing in food. You might not be able to eat the best steak in NYC or drive the best car, but with pizza you can eat the best there is for $15, and even a lot less when it's offered by the slice. People like to be able to say they've had the best.

www.PAULIEGEE.COM/SLICE-SHOP/

Hellboy

Crushed tomatoes, Grande mozzarella & Ezzo pepperoni with a drizzle of hot honey

Sausage

Crushed tomatoes, Grande mozzarella & Ezzo sliced sausage

Cheese

Crushed tomatoes & Grande mozzarella

Freddy Prince

Slow cooked tomato sauce, fresh & low moisture mozzarella with a dusting of pecorino romano on a sesame seed crust

Sharing out slices from Forcella Pizza to random New Yorkers.

Pizza Pop Culture Moments

These are the real movie stars...

HOME ALONE – 'KEEP THE CHANGE YOU FİLTHY ANİMAL'

This is it. This is the one. The most gloriously thought out and well executed pizza scene of them all. It just involves super-human VHS manipulation, and yes, the TV probably couldn't have delivered the sound quality you would need to actually pull this off, but this is just nitpicking – it's a classic scene. A young Kevin, forgotten about by his family who've gone on holiday to France, is hungry and home alone. He orders a pizza from Little Nero's and, to conceal his age from the pizza delivery boy, uses the dialogue from a gangster movie to complete the transaction. The black-and-white film that Kevin executes this with, *Angels with Filthy Souls*, was made exclusively for the movie. There is even a sequel in *Home Alone II – Angels with Even Filthier Souls*. But the best part is the end of the scene, when the driver speeds off, wheels skidding, and leaves Kevin with that inimitable feeling – 'A lovely cheese pizza – just for me.'

BREAKİNG BAD – PİZZA ON THE ROOF

In the third season of *Breaking Bad*, Walter comes home with a pizza for the family like any good dad might. In a rather less strong demonstration of paternal care, he is also cooking meth for a living. Having just discovered this, his wife refuses to let him into the house, leaving him standing on the drive with the pizza in his hands. So, in his rage, he throws the whole pizza on the roof. There has been much fan debate about how this could actually happen, as surely the pizza would be sliced, so couldn't end up on the roof in one piece. But the show tackles that head on in a later episode when Badger explains that Venezia's (the name of the pizzeria) don't cut their pizzas so they can 'pass the savings on to their customer'. So, as usual, the producers had already thought about it. In one of the great examples of life-imitating-art-imitating-life, owners of the real house where the scene was shot have had to build a fence around the property in order to prevent people from throwing pizzas on their roof.

SPACEBALLS – PİZZA THE HUTT

Probably the only pizza scene that will actively stop you from wanting to eat pizza, this classic character from Mel Brooks' *Star Wars* parody is a truly disgusting sight to behold. This really is a case of 'a picture tells a thousand words', so we won't go on, but hats off to the creative brilliance of taking the word 'Hutt', of Jabba fame, and immediately jumping to Pizza Hut. Class.

THE OFFICE – PİZZA KİDNAP

This clip is great, because it demonstrates the inevitable clash when you suggest ordering pizza to a large group. Which is the best pizza place to order from? This question inevitably raises some deep-seated emotions which we see from Kevin's comment, 'Their pizza is like eating a hot circle of garbage.' The scene also plays on the similarity in the names of so many pizza joints – the classic example in NYC is Ray's (with Ray's Pizza, Famous Ray's, Original Ray's, or Famous Original Ray's causing confusion for many a local and tourist alike). The key takeaway though? Whether you prefer Alfredo's Pizza Cafe, or Pizza by Alfredo, you should never ever kidnap the pizza boy for a discount. And if you do, maybe leave more than a two-dollar tip.

TEENAGE MUTANT NİNJA TURTLES – SEWER PİZZA DELİVERY

We should begin here with a brief history of Domino's 30-minute guarantee. Started in 1984, this tantalising offer promised that if your pizza did not arrive in half an hour then it would be free. Speed is top priority for home delivery – when you want pizza you want it now – and the speed promise is often linked to the fast growth of Domino's in the mid-eighties. The promise was downgraded to a $3 price reduction in 1986, which still seems pretty fair. However, the promise was rescinded in the early nineties – correctly we might add – when it was attributed to dangerous driving and numerous accidents involving Domino's delivery drivers frantically trying to get their pizza delivered on time (not, as the company pointed out, that the drivers were ever fined for late delivery themselves). Obviously, peoples' safety comes above pizza. This *Teenage Mutant Ninja Turtles* scene hinges entirely on that 30-minute promise, with Michelangelo waiting and hoping that his delivery will come late. It has so many great moments, from the sliding of the pizza through the sewer grate, to the classic quote – 'Wise men say forgiveness is divine, but never pay full price for late pizza' – to the ninja-style slicing and dicing of the pizza in mid-air.

SEINFELD

Our favourite in the list of business ideas that Kramer has come up with, and certainly one that we think would fly – 'make your own pie' is inspired. The real excellence of this scene is the exploration of the idea, 'when is a pizza not a pizza?'. Is it a pizza before the oven or only after it has been baked? Will certain toppings render it not a pizza? (Certainly, the Neapolitan Pizza Association would support that theory.) Either way, it is a perfect encapsulation of why pizza has endured – because the people who make it more often than not see it as more than 'just a pizza'. It is a way of life; something that cannot be entrusted to any one person to do correctly. And to be fair, cucumber on a pizza is just gross.

BACK TO THE FUTURE PART II

A nice bit of product placement for Pizza Hut here, celebrating the idea that in the future, pizzas are delivered in miniature and then enlarged in your very own rehydrator. While it is a fun concept, and certainly our favourite scene from the movie when we were kids, maybe the idea of rehydration on closer inspection feels less appetising than we thought when we were eight years old. Sadly, we checked our local electronics store in 2015, and rehydrators are still very much on the maybe pile (alongside hoverboards, flying cars and time travel in general).

ALONG CAME POLLY

Secretly one of our favourite movies – and made great by the inimitable Philip Seymour Hoffman – the 'blotting the grease' scene in this film is a classic moment in pizza pop culture. It's a brilliant way to highlight the difference between the carefree Sandy and worrying Reuben, and it does actually highlight a key pizza question. Is the grease a key part of the experience or not?

FRIENDS

Friends is awash with pizza – they are in the heart of NYC after all – and it particularly celebrates the use of pizza as a classic post-breakup pick-me-up. However, our favourite scene, which isn't really about pizza at all, is when Ross tries to flirt with the pizza delivery girl. Ross, first off, is clearly the best character in *Friends*. It would be nothing without Ross (see 'paste pants', 'MY sandwich', 'I'm fiiiiiine'). But this scene is one of the best, most awkward TV moments out there. 'Intense.' Worth noting that *Friends* is also responsible for another global phenomenon, 'The Joey Special' – two pizzas!

FAST TİMES AT RİDGEMONT HİGH

Arguably the movie that invented the teen comedy, *Fast Times at Ridgemont High* feels tame these days, but at the time of its release it caused real shockwaves. And what's more, it has pizza at the very heart of it – Perry's Pizza was the pizza place that Jennifer Jason Leigh and Phoebe Cates worked at (the former even got a job there in real life in a slightly over-the-top method acting move). However, the pizza scene that steals the show is when Spicoli, the surf dude played by Sean Penn, gets a pizza delivered to class. His logic is flawless, and really, he causes no disturbance at all. But the unwritten teacher law says that pizza cannot be delivered to class, and so his meal gets distributed between the other students. We still feel like this is a key part of what is wrong with the universe.

THE NET – SANDRA BULLOCK

Unlike *Back to the Future Part II*, whose version of the future never really materialised, *The Net* was actually bang on the money. When it came out in 1995, the internet was in its early CompuServe-based infancy. The idea of ordering a real-life pizza to your door without even speaking to a human was full-on sci-fi. Yet here we are, able to order a pizza from our watch if we want. It's amazing to think that something so commonplace today was, only 25 years ago, a total pipe dream. Fair to say the slightly ropey animated fireplace in the same scene hasn't been quite as popular an invention (although you can watch a burning log fire on Netflix now for when you need some comfort on those long, cold winter nights).

SATURDAY NİGHT FEVER – TONY 'TWO SLİCE' MANERO

Probably one of the most iconic movie openings of all time is when John Travolta struts to Brooklyn in time to that classic Bee Gees soundtrack carrying a can of paint. The effortless stop off at Lenny's Pizzeria (still there in Brooklyn if you fancy a visit) to pick up two slices of pizza (not three – that would be silly) is iconic. How do you eat those two slices of pizza when you have nowhere to leave your paint? Double decker style of course! Absolutely legendary. Turns out, this is not a standard Brooklyn thing. So, the creation of the double decker slice is a 100%, solid gold, Tony Manero original. And all the better for it. Ingenious.

'ANYONE WHO SAYS THAT MONEY CANNOT BUY HAPPiNESS HAS CLEARLY NEVER SPENT THEiR MONEY ON PiZZA.'

ANDREW W.K.

Making NY Slice Pizza at Home

Growing up, New York slice pizza was the food from movies that we most craved. The pepperoni pies delivered by April to the turtles in the sewers, the pizza delivered by Peter Parker, the pizza Rachel orders when she finds out Ross slept with the copy girl. There's something about the NY slice that is so unfussy, that it is the perfect pizza to eat on the sofa while binge-watching *Stranger Things*. (Best. Show. Ever.) Here's our method for recreating this cult classic.

THE DOUGH

650g (4⅔ cups) strong white bread flour, plus extra for dusting

1½ tbsp sugar

3 tsp sea salt

2 tsp instant yeast

450ml (scant 2 cups) lukewarm water

3 tbsp extra-virgin olive oil

THE SAUCE

good-quality olive oil

2 garlic cloves, chopped

2 x 400g (14oz) cans good-quality plum tomatoes

a good pinch each of salt, pepper and sugar

a good pinch of dried oregano

a handful of chopped basil

THE TOPPING

semi-dry grated mozzarella (placed in the freezer for 20 minutes)

METHOD

1. Mix the flour, sugar, salt and yeast in a food processor. Quickly pulse until the ingredients are incorporated. Add the water and olive oil, then pulse until the dough forms a ball that rides around the bowl above the blade, about 30 seconds.

2. Knead the dough on a lightly floured surface until smooth. Divide the dough into two even balls and pop into two individual freezer bags. Place in the fridge and allow to prove for at least 24–48 hours.

3. Heat a glug of olive oil in a saucepan. Add the garlic and gently fry until golden brown. Add the tomatoes, salt, pepper, sugar, oregano and basil. Gently cook the tomato sauce with a lid on for 1 hour until the tomatoes have broken down and you have a deep-flavoured sauce. Leave to cool.

4. Two hours before you're ready for pizza, take the dough out the fridge and shape into balls by gathering the dough towards the bottom and pinching it. Flour well and place each ball in a separate bowl. Cover tightly with clingfilm (plastic wrap) and allow to rise in a warm spot until doubled in size.

5. One hour before pizza time, preheat your oven as hot as it will go. Place a pizza stone or baking sheet in the oven.

6. Stretch one of your dough balls into a circle, into a 14-inch base, leaving a 1-inch crust. Transfer to a chopping board.

7. Spoon half the sauce onto your base and evenly spread, avoiding the crust. Top with some semi-frozen mozzarella.

8. Slide your pizza into the oven and cook for 10–12 minutes until the crust is browned and the cheese has melted. Slice.

9. Repeat with the other dough ball and remaining sauce and mozzarella.

PIZZA PILGRIMS CITY GUIDE

NEW HAVEN

A Darwinian experiment to create a unique pizza.

Given that New Haven is only about 80 miles from New York, it really is surprising that its pizza culture was not consumed by The Big Apple at the turn of the 20th century. Both locations had seen a large number of immigrants coming over the water from Naples looking for work and, once these people realised that their future might be pizza-less in the USA, they quickly got on to making sure that was not the case. However, as it stands, pizza in New Haven is a completely unique thing – and a thing of beauty at that. For starters, it is not called pizza, but 'apizza' – this harks back to the Italian *a pizza* (meaning 'the pizza'). Secondly, there are ten unique qualities of New Haven pizza that set it apart from the rest of the pizza world. Learn them, then make the pilgrimage...

PLAIN PIES

New Haven has a different take on the plain pie than elsewhere in the US. Ever since the birth of New Haven pizza with the opening of Frank Pepe in 1925, the plain pie has remained as simple as can be. Just tomato sauce, oregano and a sprinkling of pecorino romano cheese on the top. It is totally delicious, but can feel a little sparse if you aren't expecting it. You will feel like a legit local though.

MOZZARELLA

More legit stuff here. If you want mozzarella on your pizza you have to request it specially. And if you really want to sound like a local, you have to refer to it as 'mootz'. It's a hard one to pull off...

Zuppardi's, home of the best clam pie in New Haven. These two have been coming here every Thursday for 23 years.

Embracing the uneven slicing at Sally's in New Haven.

COAL

The pizza ovens in New Haven are totally unique. They are 100% powered by coal and they are huge – almost like a room in themselves. That means you need pizza peels that are five metres long to move the pizzas around, and a team of people in the kitchen who have a sixth sense for dodging these peels as they whip around the kitchen. Like a little pizza ballet 24 hours a day! The ovens themselves get up to high temperatures around 350°C/660°F and they stay on all the time. It takes a week to get them back up to temperature when the stores close for a refurb!

SLICING

As a mark of democracy, pies in New Haven are not cut into equal slices. Instead, once the pie arrives at your table, it is basically attacked by your server, who cuts it into a mishmash of different sized slices. This is done to make sure people are getting what they want – smaller slices for kids, larger slices for the grown-ups; you get the picture. It actually makes loads of sense, even if it might cause more family trauma than necessary.

CLAMS

The big man Frank Pepe was the first person to take the leap of putting clams onto his pizza – and it has remained a sure-fire hit ever since. Clams are a local delicacy and they have really taken off as a topping at almost all the big pizzerias in New Haven. Be warned: clam pies are packed with garlic, so are not great first-date fodder. Also – as a little tip – make sure you try the clam pie at Zuppardi's in West Haven (about 10 minutes' drive). It's the best we've tasted!

HISTORY

New Haven is a town with a lot of history (it is the home to Yale University, after all) and that is true of its pizza as well! Frank Pepe was an Italian immigrant who moved to New Haven in 1909. After the First World War, when he nobly returned to Italy to fight for his homeland, he came back to the US and took a job in a local bakery in Wooster Street. While working there he developed his famous 'tomato pies' and started selling them at the local market. They were such a success that soon enough he took over the bakery he was working in, opening Frank Pepe Pizzeria Napoletana in June 1925. To put this into context, in 1925 you would have found very few pizzerias in Italy outside of Naples, so this really is a historical location. There was a bit of to-ing and fro-ing over the coming century, and Frank himself died in 1969 (around the time the Beatles broke up…), but the pizzeria still trades from (essentially) the same location as it opened almost 100 years ago.

SHAPE

New Haven pizzas are a celebration of wonkiness, and the shape is totally endearing. They are not square, but not circular – they look like factory seconds! But once you take that first bite, all shape-based concerns melt away.

LINGO

It's worth reiterating that New Haven pizza has a language all of its own. You can try your best to fit in with the locals, or just play dumb and let some nice person take pity on you. Things to look out for include:

Tomato pie: the plain pizzas served in all of New Haven

Mootz: the local term for mozzarella

Foxton Park: the local soda that is synonymous with soft drinks in New Haven

Apizza: the local name for pizza.

CHAR

Probably the most important thing to remember in New Haven is that their pizza is not burned! It is 'charred'. And it is an essential part of the taste of New Haven pizza! Now stop complaining and get eating.

THE HOLY TRINITY

So, New Haven's legendary pizzerias are kind of like London Buses – they all come along at once. In this case, the three most legendary pizzerias in New Haven all opened inside of 13 years. Frank Pepe kicked it off in 1925, followed by Modern Apizza in 1934 and Sally's in 1938. And since then, no new pizzerias have come up to meet this hallowed trio. All three are still trading today and all are still as excellent as they were when they started out. So here, in short, is a mini review of each:

SALLY'S APIZZA

To us, Sally's is all about the vibe. The pizza is great, of course, but it is the energy and warmth in the place that really makes it special. It has a really homely feel, with many of the team having worked there for decades, and it has a very 'lived in' atmosphere. Sally's creates probably our favourite New Haven plain pie, but it was the first one we ever tried, so we might be biased.

MODERN APIZZA

You'll find that Modern has the best reviews online for its pizza – and we have to say that it is truly great. The Italian bomb is a thing of beauty! The team are friendly and efficient and it is great to see a mother/father/daughter team all working alongside each other.

FRANK PEPE

The place that started it all – and a total must visit! The team are so friendly and the pies really feel like the most authentic of the New Haven pizzas we've tried. Make sure you have the clam pie with bacon! And for a fully legit experience, try to get a seat in 'The Spot' (over the road from the main pizzeria and the place where it really all began).

The legendary coal oven at Frank Pepe.

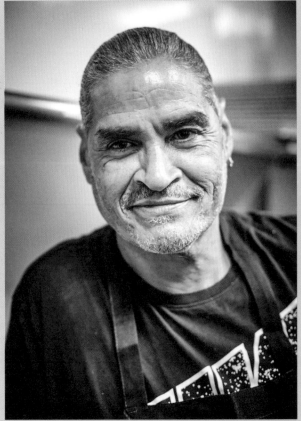

Always buckle up when eating Zuppardi's legendary clam pie!

The World Pizza Games

Essentially Top Gun for pizza makers.

The World Pizza Games are held at the Pizza Expo in March every year in Las Vegas. The Games focus on the skill of manipulating dough, rather than any taste or creative challenges. This obviously makes sense, as the tests end up being less subjective than they might have otherwise been. In order to take part, you have to work in a pizzeria or in the world of pizza, so this is strictly for the true professionals. The competition has a real feeling of a Pizza Olympics – last year over 10,000 people watched the games unfold. For a bit more about the games see our interview with Tony Gemignani on page 250. For now, let us take you through the five categories of the competition in a little more detail:

FREESTYLE ACROBATIC DOUGH TOSSING

For the true show-boaters, this contest is basically the pizza equivalent of *Bring it On* or *Strictly Come Dancing*. Contestants are required to come up with their own routine, including the music of course, to be scored by a panel of judges. The panel are looking for things like dexterity, difficulty level of tricks undertaken, and entertainment value, but contestants need to be careful not to drop their dough or they will lose points. It's hard to convey the spectacle of this in a book, so it's definitely worth getting on YouTube to check this out.

There are two contests within this challenge – one for the standard pizza professional, and one for 'Masters' who have won the competition (or a similar one) before. It really is deadly serious – being a Master competitor here is a true honour.

FASTEST DOUGH

This is essentially a test to see how quickly you can turn a pre-prepared ball of dough into a pizza base ready for topping. Contestant pizzaioli are presented with five balls of dough on a bed of flour and have to throw them into five pizza bases as quickly as possible. The judges are on hand to check that each pizza base covers a dedicated size marker entirely, and that any holes larger than a pencil are fully repaired. This happens fast (clue's in the name), with the record currently set at 23.04 seconds by a 2016 contestant – that's under five seconds for each individual base.

LARGEST DOUGH STRETCH

Again, the clue is the name for this one. Essentially, competitors have five minutes to make a pizza base of the largest possible diameter from a 500g (1lb 2oz) ball of dough. Individual pizzaioli can only use their hands (helpfully the rules state that you cannot use your legs, feet or head) but they do have the option of preparing the base on a table or in the air, before placing it on the floor for judging. With contestants regularly stretching the base to over 1m/3ft – creating a pizza base that is basically thin enough to see through – the strict rule of 'no holes larger than a pencil' really starts to become a challenge!

FASTEST PIZZA BOX FOLDING

The contestants have to fold five standard 12-inch pizza boxes from flat-pack to ready-to-hold-pizza. We actually hold a version of this competition at our annual staff party, so we can confirm that the record of just over 20 seconds is very, very fast.

PIZZA TRIATHLON

A subtle combination of some of the above games, the triathlon involves folding one pizza box, then stretching two 22oz balls of dough into 16-inch and 22-inch pizza bases in the fastest time. We're fans of this challenge because it's a nice balance of both front-of-house and back-of-house skills – bringing the two worlds together.

Pizza World Records

Harder, Better, Faster, Stronger (ish)

The human race is remarkable. Really, it is. We are dedicating real time to breaking pizza records, while the world has a few, slightly more pressing things to attend to. That said, you can't help but be amazed by some of these!

LONGEST PIZZA

The longest pizza ever was made in Fontana, California, on 10 June 2017. It measured 1,930.39m long – that's 1.3 miles! We just really hope that it was eaten afterwards rather than thrown away.

LARGEST PIZZA

The largest pizza ever made was created in Rome in December 2012. It measured 1,261.65m squared. To put that in context, a tennis court is only 261m squared – so it was the size of FIVE tennis courts. Ace.

LONGEST PIZZA FRITTA

The longest fried pizza on record was made by legendary pizza company Rossopomodoro in Naples on 23 May 2018. There were 60 dedicated pizzaioli involved in the project and its final length was 7.15m (23.5ft). A dedicated pan was made containing 1,500 litres of vegetable oil to do the deep frying in!

CHEESIEST PIZZA

The pizza with the most varieties of cheese on it was achieved by Johnny di Francesco at 400 Gradi pizzeria in Melbourne – topping out at 154 varieties!

FURTHEST PIZZA DELIVERY

Paul Fenech hand-delivered a pizza a cool 12,346.6 miles in June and July 2006 from Wellington, New Zealand to Madrid in Spain. We are assuming it was cold on delivery.

Special mention also goes to Pizza Hut in South Africa, who delivered a pizza to the highest recorded point – 5,897m at the top of Mount Kilimanjaro in May 2016.

LARGEST COLLECTION OF PIZZA BOXES

Scott Wiener in New York City – who runs the now-legendary Scott's Pizza Tours – has amassed the largest collection of legit and individual pizzas boxes. He's even taken his pizza box collection on tour to a number of cities around the world. See our interview with Scott on page 204.

MOST PIZZAS MADE IN ONE HOUR

Domino's (not unsurprisingly) have this one sewn up, with Brian Edler making 206 pizzas in one hour in Ohio.

LARGEST PIZZA BASE SPINNING

Tony Gemignani (13-time world pizza champion) managed to spin 500g (18oz) of pizza dough for 2 minutes to form a pizza base measuring 84.33cm (33.2in) across in Minneapolis in 2006.

FASTEST PİZZA EATİNG

Kelvin Medina from the Philippines ate a 12-inch pizza with a knife and fork in 23.62 seconds – the guy in second place was only half a second behind. His big tip? 'You have to bite, then swallow, then bite, then swallow.' Got it.

Joey Chestnut ate 40½ slices of Pizza Hut pizza in December 2017 to win a separate, volume-related World Record.

LONGEST CALZONE

18.22m (about 60ft) is the longest calzone ever made – created in Ontario, Canada. You could get three people into it head to toe if you wanted to...

PİZZA BOX TOWER

The tallest tower constructed from cardboard pizza boxes was 'The Leaning Tower of Pizza', erected at the Carousel Hotel, Ocean City, Delaware, on 31 August 1996. It was 11.1m high.

	ACROBATIC DOUGH TOSSING (MASTERS)	FREESTYLE AROBATIC DOUGH TOSSING	FASTEST DOUGH	LARGEST DOUGH STRETCH	FASTEST PIZZA BOX FOLDING	PIZZA TRIATHLON
2019 GOLD MEDALLIST	Lee Moon, Mr Pizza	Juntae Jin, Mr Pizza	Mitch Rotolo Jr., Rotolo's Pizza	Nathan Wilson, Six Hundred Downtown	James Riley, Sexy Pizza	Mitch Rotolo Jr., Rotolo's Pizza
2018 GOLD MEDALLIST	Scott Volpe, Fiamme Pizza Napoletana	Ezequiel Ortigoza, Association Pizzeros Argentina	Mitch Rotolo Jr., Rotolo's Pizza	Salvatore Salviviani, Pizzeria L'Angolo Di Langhirano	Zolbayar Ganbold, Cousin Vinny's Pizza	Mitch Rotolo Jr., Rotolo's Pizza
2017 GOLD MEDALLIST	Justin Waldstein, Pizza My Heart	Scott Volpe, Fiamme Pizza	Mitch Rotolo Jr., Rotolo's Pizza	Matt Hickey, Caliente Pizza & Draft House	Bonn Rassavong, Citizen Pie	Justin Waldstein, Pizza My Heart
2016 GOLD MEDALLIST	Jay Schurman, Pizza Rock	Hyeonsoo Joo, Mr. Pizza	Mitch Rotolo Jr., Rotolo's Pizza	Carlos Mangana, Pizza My Heart	David Whisker, B.C. Pizza	Justin Waldstein, Pizza My Heart
2015 GOLD MEDALLIST	Min-Chul Shin, Mr. Pizza	Min-Chul Shin, Mr. Pizza	Brittany Saxton, Six Hundred Downtown	Spencer Glenn, Pizza My Heart	Spencer Glenn, Pizza My Heart	Dave Sommers, Mad Mushroom
2014 GOLD MEDALLIST	Justin Waldstein, Pizza My Heart	Lee Moonky	Brittany Saxton, Six Hundred Downtown	Brittany Saxton, Six Hundred Downtown	Barry White, Pizza My Heart	Justin Waldstein, Pizza My Heart
2013 GOLD MEDALLIST	Kazuya Akaogi, Red Japan Co	Eric Ross, Tony's Pizza Napoletana	Brittany Saxton, Six Hundred Downtown	Garrett Marlin, Uncle's Pizzeria & Co	Barry White, Pizza My Heart	David Whisker, B.C. Pizza

Tony Gemignani

This man has taken on everything pizza has to offer – and won.

Known as the 'Michael Jordan of pizza throwing' Tony is a thirteen-time world pizza champion and truly spins dough like no other human on the planet. In 2007 this legend was awarded the title of 'World Champion Pizza Maker' at the World Pizza Cup in Naples, which made him the first non-Neapolitan to ever win the title… MEGA. Check out our feature on not one, but two of his restaurants on page 35.

Thom+James: So Tony, why do you think pizza is something people turn to time and time again?

Tony: For me, pizza was a part of my life from a very early age. Every kid loves pizza, so, whatever is going on in your life, eating a

slice of pizza will take you back to a simpler time. It's communal and it's creative. With or without cheese, thin, thick, in a pan, wood-fired, square, round – it can be anything you want. It is synonymous with family – you grow up with pizza and you love it until the day you die.

Thom+James: Totally agree. So how did you get into pizza?

Tony: I was just getting out of high school and didn't know what I was going to do. My brother was about to open a pizzeria and he asked me if I wanted to join. Cooking was a big deal in our family – we grew up on a farm in Fremont, CA, so we were used to using our hands. My brother showed me the ropes and I just fell in love with it. My competitive streak kicked in and I became obsessed with making every pizza better than the last (and better than my brother!). From there it just snowballed.

Thom+James: Are you competitive in all areas of your life?

Tony: Yeah, I guess I am! My dad was a soccer coach, so I think my competitive streak came from him. When I started out you couldn't just Google things to find out how to get better. You had to work at it. When we opened the doors of our little independent pizzeria in the Castro Valley in California in 1991, we just had to get on with it. It was a steep learning curve. We were lucky because my brother had worked at some great pizzerias when he was younger, so he had a great foundation that he was able to teach me. But we really learned authenticity by travelling and learning in places like Naples and Rome.

Thom+James: Tell us about your current pizzeria. You celebrate pizza in every form, don't you?

Tony: Yeah, we do multiple ovens and multiple styles! I want to celebrate Naples, but I also want to celebrate Chicago, St Louis, New York… When done well, every one of those pizza styles is great. The 'old way' of pizza making is to find your niche and stick to it, but the future is about choice – and that is what the consumer wants at the end of the day.

Thom+James: So, talk to us about the Pizza Games. How did you get into that?

Tony: So, the Pizza Games started in the '80s. While I was working at the pizza shop in 1991, the guys would always talk about Barry O'Halloran (who was a big deal then – he was on *The Johnny Carson Show* so that dates it for you!) and how he did a trick called 'The Whip'. We would all try to recreate it in the pizzeria, but the guys who had worked in pizza longer than me were way better. So, being competitive, I started practising hard! I then got a chance to

go to Vegas and see the Games. I just couldn't believe the moves these guys were doing. I thought I was good, but these guys were ace! They spotted I had talent and asked me to join them, but I declined at the time. However, I decided I was going to come back the next year and win! I trained all year and it paid off, because I ended up winning the games three years in a row. I then ended up going to Italy to compete and won there two years in a row at the World Championships. Then they banned me from competing… so I became a judge.

Thom+James: What dough do you use to compete? Is it a set recipe globally for all competitors?

Tony: Good question. Back in the day there was no secret recipe. Anyone could use their own dough. But basically you want to make a dough with high protein flour, triple the salt and low hydration. It should be firm, hard, cold. No yeast. Ice cold water. Back in the day I used to use two beach towels to practice with. I cut them into circles and then stitched them together. I then slightly wet the towels to make them sag in the middle – it really closely mimicked a disc of dough!

Thom+James: OK, big questions. What's your favourite type of pizza? (We realise that this might be like asking you to pick your favourite child!)

Tony: Yeah, that's tough! I'd have to say a coal-fired pizza – I'm loving that at the moment – topped with 'nduja and arugula (rocket).

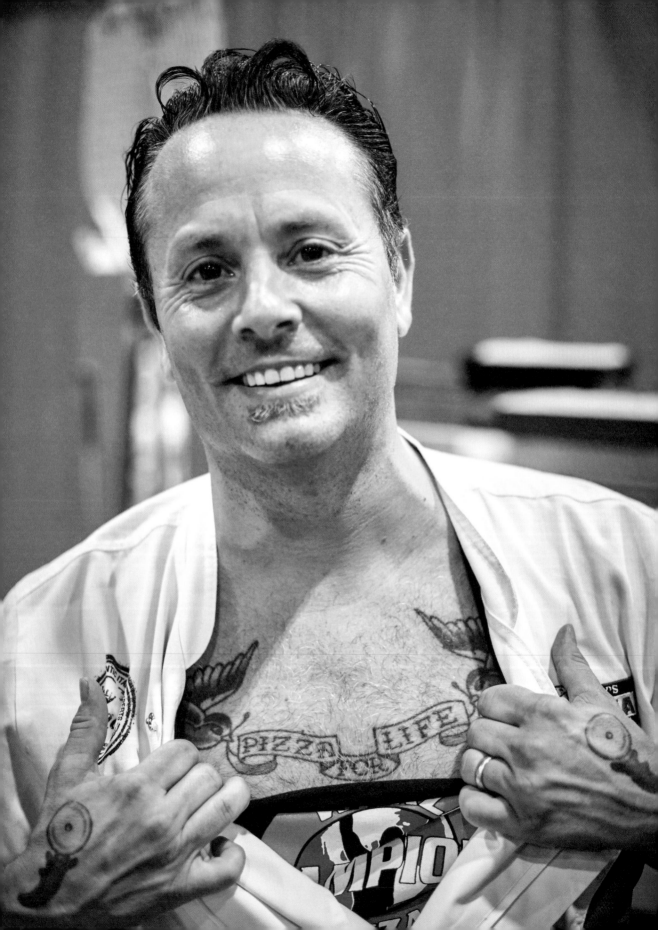

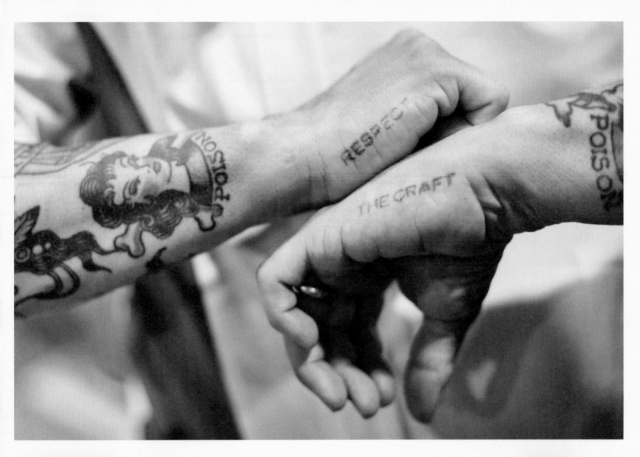

CHICAGO

It's not all about deep dish, but even if it were it would still be worth a visit!

Chicago is a town with a bit of a pizza identity crisis. Many people see deep dish as a grotesque straight-out-the-freezer-aisle monstrosity, which is to give Chicago a totally unfair dismissal in the pizza stakes. Not only can deep dish be a truly sensational product, but the city has a pizza culture with depth to match New York, and arguably variety to beat it. This city is an essential visit for the true pizza fanatic, although we'd advise you to think really (really) hard before taking it on in winter!

PEQUOD'S PIZZA

This pizzeria sits slightly out of town, but it is totally worth the journey. It has a sports bar vibe, which lends it an overwhelming sense of Americana, but do not be deceived. This place has some serious pizza. It is deep-dish style, but it has a crust unlike any other pie we have tasted in the world. Deeply caramelised in the oven, its rich, buttery taste and amazing crunch, combined with excellent ingredients, make it one of the finest pies in all of Chicago.

PIECE

One of the coolest venues in Chicago, we defy you not to have a great night in Piece. It's a huge space serving fantastic, New Haven-style pizza (see page 234), brewing their own award-winning beers and laying on a fabulous selection of bands and live acts (as well as showing all the sport you could desire). Owner Bill Jacobs has just the right amount of healthy obsession (having grown up in New Haven himself), and the pizzeria and brewery quickly rose to fame when they employed two members of MTV's *The Real World: Chicago*. The young team and clientele make you feel like you are in an American sitcom (in a good way) and a night out here is not to be missed in Chicago. Oh, and trust us, get the clam pizza. You can thank us later.

COALFIRE

Dave at Coalfire runs a tight pizza ship built on real passion and a fantastic thin crust. No prizes for guessing that the pizzas are baked in coal-fired, super-hot ovens, producing a blistered, super-thin yet chewy crust that really is to die for. But it's the topping combinations that really take this place to the next level. The ingredients are always locally sourced and well combined, and the addition of whipped ricotta is a stroke of genius. The pepperoni and the Ezzo are worth the journey alone.

SPACCA NAPOLI

Surely the most popular name for a Neapolitan pizzeria worldwide, this spot is named after the historic street that crosses the old town in Naples – and it really does channel Italy. Spacca Napoli serves fantastic, authentic Neapolitan pizza and, with an amazing oven and piazza to match, you can tell they really care about what they do.

GINO'S EAST

The second place to open in Chicago serving deep-dish pizza, this place has really stood the test of time. The pies are all still fantastic and, in their words, #deepAF. Gino's have a number of pizzerias across Chicago and the US now, and all the locations have really embraced the Chicago Brew Pub culture, providing great home-brewed beers to wash down your pie. One thing to keep in mind with deep dish is that it takes a LONG time to make – around 35 minutes minimum from the time of order. So, on that basis, it's important to have great beer on tap to keep you ticking over during the wait! Top tip: Gino's East will literally ship you a frozen pie if you can't quite make it down to the Windy City!

CHICAGO PIZZA AND OVEN GRINDER CO.

Throughout all our pizza travels, of all the pizzerias we have visited and all the different styles of pizza we have tried, we can honestly say that Chicago Pizza and Oven Grinder Co. serves the maddest pizza we have ever experienced. From the moment you walk through the door, you're met with a huge queue and one man in charge of it all (with no pen or paper, just a photographic memory) telling you to wait and he will seat you in order. You don't believe him, but miraculously he reappears and your table is suddenly ready. What awaits you next? The pizza. It is baked in an upside-down bowl (kind of like a pot pie) with the pizza 'toppings' inside the bowl, and the crust on top sealing everything inside. At your table the dish is then turned out onto a plate, so that the pizza is now the right way up. We're not gonna lie, it kind of looks like something that has just been given birth to. It is mental. We were so bewildered (and a little drunk) at the time, that we honestly can't tell you if it tasted good or not. But you just have to go, because you won't experience anything like it anywhere else.

LOU MALNATİ'S

Part of the select few places that claim to have access to the original recipe of deep-dish pizza, Lou Malnati's now has more than 50 locations – all in high-footfall areas and with a very strong brand feel – and is a force to be reckoned with. Because of this, we were expecting the quality to be lacking, but actually, the deep dish is really great, with a buttery crust and lashings of cheese, sausage and tomato. The surroundings are rather uninspiring, but the pizza is definitely worth checking out. And make sure you get the cookie dough pudding – it's something else.

PİZANO'S

Another location claiming to have a direct link to the original recipe of deep-dish pizza (and run by the supposed inventor's wife and son), Pizano's is another large chain with great pizza. It's so good, in fact, that they claim to be Oprah Winfrey's favourite pizzeria! This is a fantastic place to try deep dish the way it was intended, but they also offer up great thin-crust pizzas too – you really can't go wrong here.

UNO PİZZERİA

This is the place to visit for a slice of pizza history. Although, you might be better off just watching someone else eat the pizza... The place is quite tired, the pizza isn't the best but, while it doesn't live up to some of the other places on this list, we've included it because of the significant role it's played in Chicago's pizza heritage. It is the birthplace of deep dish, after all – and that's got to be worth a beer at the bar if nothing else.

Deep dish's first pizzeria –
so important it gets its own plaque.

Outside Piece Pizzeria with owners
Bill and John – local pizza heroes.

Chicago Deep Dish Pizza

Undeniably delish, if not exactly light.

Chicago is, in its own way, as obsessed with pizza as New York. Hit by the same Italian immigration influx in the late 1800s and early 1900s, the streets of Chicago are awash with pizzerias serving all kinds of pizza, from thin crust, to thick crust, to tavern style.

It is, however, the 'deep dish' that has captured the imagination of the world, and it is undoubtedly a departure from pizza as we know it. More pie that pizza, it turns almost everything you know about pizza on its head.

To add to the bizarreness, this 'hearty' dish was actually made popular by a sportsman. American footballer Ike Sewell, along with restaurateur Ric Riccardo, opened Pizzeria Uno in 1943. It served a new, cake-like version of pizza brimming with cheese, tomato, sausage and onion – a dish to match the bitter winters of Chicago. Pizzeria Uno is still there to this day, although it's probably fair to say that the history of the place is more impressive than its pizza.

The story actually goes deeper (pun intended) than that, though, because despite Ike and Ric gaining a lot of the plaudits for inventing deep dish, a chef at Uno, Rudy Malnati Sr., is the man who actually claimed to have invented the dish himself – it was apparently only later that Ike and Ric came onto the scene (see page 256).

And, to be fair to the Malnati family, their version of events does carry some weight, especially as they've gone on to dominate the Chicago pizza scene. Working with his son Lou, Rudy stayed at Pizzeria Uno perfecting 'his' recipe until his death. At this point, Lou left Uno and started the now ubiquitous Lou Malnati's in 1971. There are now more than 50 pizzerias operating under that name in the Chicago area, serving their famous 'buttercrust' version of the deep dish. In a further twist, and intriguing to us as brothers, Lou's half-brother Rudy Jr. started a competing chain, Pizano, in the 1990s (and what's more, he claims that only he had the secret recipe originally developed by Rudy Sr. back in 1943).

There are, of course, many places serving deep dish now but one other place worth a special mention (and which has no part to play in the 'Malnati Trilogy') is Gino's East. Only the second pizzeria to open serving deep dish in 1966, it is still family owned and one of the best exponents of the craft in the city. We collaborated with them in 2018 to bring their unique take on deep-dish pizza to the terrace of our pizzeria in London. It was a triumphant affair, and even in the height of mid-summer their pizzas went down a treat.

We have teamed up with Gino's again to bring you a recipe for their famous pie, so you can have a crack at trying one of the best deep-dish pizzas in Chicago!

INGREDIENTS

1 tsp granulated sugar

2¼ tsp active dry yeast

500g (18oz) plain (all-purpose) flour

75g (2¾oz) polenta (cornmeal)

2 tsp fine sea salt

3 tbsp olive oil, plus extra for greasing

1 tbsp unsalted butter, melted

350g (12oz) mozzarella, sliced

450g (1lb) raw Italian sausage, thinly sliced

225g (8oz) pepperoni, thinly sliced

2 x 400g (14oz) cans whole San Marzano tomatoes, crushed by hand

Parmesan, for grating

METHOD

1. Mix the sugar, yeast and 300ml (11fl oz) room-temperature water in a bowl and allow to 'bloom' for 15 minutes. Combine the flour, polenta and salt in the bowl of a stand mixer. Once the yeast has bloomed, add to the dry ingredients along with olive oil. Gently combine until a rough ball is formed.

2. Knead on low speed with the dough hook for 90 seconds. Transfer to a lightly oiled bowl and prove until doubled in size, about 6 hours. Knock back the dough, then let it rest for 15 minutes.

3. Position an oven rack in the middle of the oven and preheat to 230°C/450°F/ Gas 8.

4. Coat the bottom and sides of a 12-inch cake pan or traditional Chicago-style pizza pan with the melted butter. Using your hands, spread out about three quarters of the dough across the bottom and up the sides of the pan (save the remainder for another use). Cover the entire base in mozzarella, all the way up to the edge. Cover half with a thin, even layer of the raw Italian sausage. Cover the other half with the pepperoni. Top with a couple of handfuls of crushed tomatoes, spreading to the edges, then sprinkle the top with grated Parmesan.

5. Bake in the hot oven, rotating halfway through, until golden around the edge, about 25 minutes. Leave to rest for 5 minutes or so, then either gently lift the pizza out of the pan or just cut your slice directly from the pan.

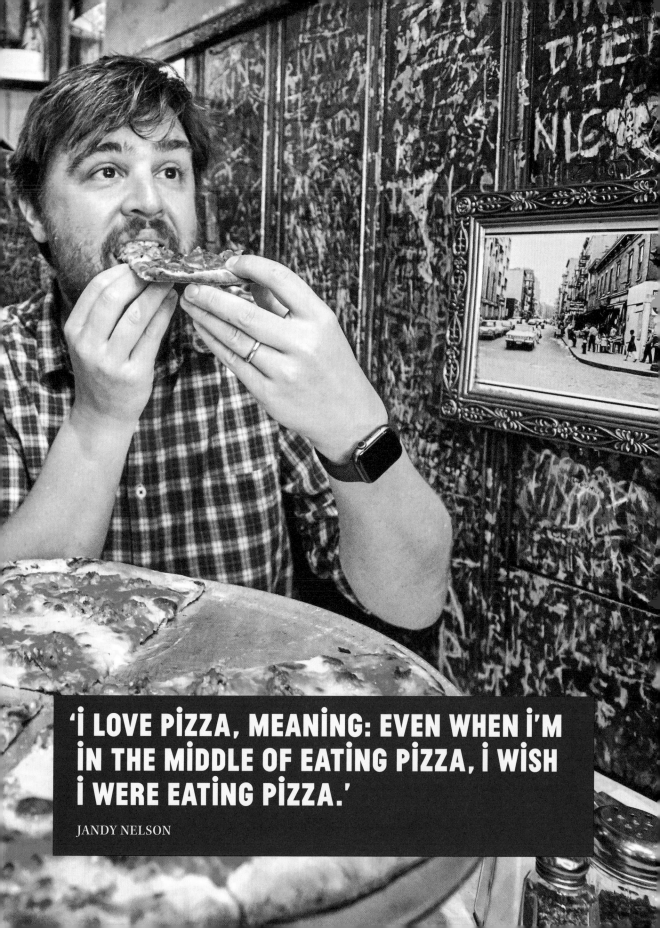

'I LOVE PİZZA, MEANİNG: EVEN WHEN İ'M İN THE MİDDLE OF EATİNG PİZZA, İ WİSH İ WERE EATİNG PİZZA.'

JANDY NELSON

The Final Slice...

Well folks, that right there is just about everything we know about pizza... so far. We are sitting at Thom's kitchen table with this book designed and laid out in front of us. It's a very surreal experience to have the last 9 years of your life laid out neatly in a book for you to peruse. Maybe we could have done more with our time? Become doctors or lawyers, or maybe adventure-seeking archaeologists with bullwhips, fedora hats and satchels? (Sorry, childhood ambitions there...)

But no, the pizza life is the life for us. It's taken us all over the world, from Chicago to Abu Dhabi, Beirut to Rome, and has allowed us to meet the most incredible community of people. From the 85-year-old buffalo mozzarella farmer and his wife that we met at the beginning of our pilgrimage, who swore the key to a happy life was a glass of freshly squeezed donkey milk every morning, to Jens Hofma, the CEO of Pizza Hut who believes that people love pizza because it's round and unthreatening. It's fair to say that pizza is a global passion that attracts all walks of life into its doughy circle of crust.

It is hard to imagine a food that is more joyful, inclusive and wide reaching. We made a point of asking every single person we met while writing this book what they thought it was about pizza that people love so much. The answer to that question can be boiled down to the simple idea that pizza is something that you can depend on in an ever more complicated world. Whether you're going though a painful breakup, or you've overexerted yourself the night before, or you're suffering from a bout of homesickness, pizza is a dish that always delivers the goods. Be it a stuffed crust, a double-decadence meat feast from Domino's, or a puritanical Marinara from Da Michele, every pizza has its place, and they all do their part in creating a happier world. We suppose what we're trying to say is: **pizza is happiness.**

James Thom

Index

Thanks

How the stuffed crust do you thank everyone that's been part of our pizza journey so far? It's impossible. Which is why the first thanks goes to all the people we have forgotten. Our bad – we were in a pizza coma at the time.

Jemma and Lena, thank you for putting up with us NEVER SHUTTING UP about pizza. It must be a daily struggle, but you put a ring on it. Jackson and Sadie, thanks for telling us 'Daddy's pizza is the best!'.

Vicky and Shirl for being our biggest fans and bringing us up on Domino's and Goodfella's frozen pizza.

Everyone in the Pizza Pilgrims Family – now and in the past. We are constantly amazed at the love and level of dedication you all bring to serving up some of the best pizza in London. Bring on another 10 years!

Team book, what can we say; we've loved it! Thank you for making this such a fun-filled and creative process! Sarah, for first meeting us for that BBQ pizza in Cambridge and believing in the idea. Harriet, for embracing the world of pizza so fundamentally, being such a joy to work with and keeping that word count down! Claire, for keeping this design on track – who says a mad-capped scrapbook about pizza can't be beautiful?!

Dave! Dave, Dave, Dave… It's been emotional mate. You are hands down the best photographer in the biz and your dedication to getting shots of pizza ovens, pizzas, hands picking up pizza, hands putting down pizza, pizza signage, pizza cheese pulls and pizza-covered pizza makers is second to none. And then to be a designer too! It's sickening! Let's see if we can get a second book off the ground and keep travelling the world of pizza! (Also, sorry again for pushing you into the bins in New York…)

Giuseppe, George, Laura, Henry, Nick, Debbie, James, Fabrizio – our amazing suppliers who help us source everything we need to bring the pizza to the people. You guys are the heroes!

To the *ragazzi* in Naples, who have made us feel welcome the last 27 times we've been in the crazy city: Antimo Caputo, Giovanni Amodio, Ciro Oliva, Alessandro Condurro, Gino Sorbillo, Vincenzo Capuano… *FORZA NAPOLI!*

Scott, Paulie, Steph, Bill – our pizza correspondents in NYC. The New York pizza scene is hard to beat for passion, community, sense of humour and just full-blown American eccentricity. I hope you take it as a compliment that we put you all firmly in that category.

And to our local slice of the pizza scene in London. Pasquale and Angelo from Santa Maria, Mark and Ry from Homeslice, Nick and Johnnie at Yard Sale, Silvestro from Sud Italia, Dan from Voodoo Ray's, and, of course, the one, the only Daniel Young. You all bring something to the table which puts the London pizza scene up there with the best of them!

And finally to our amazing customers who have kept us in the biz through the past 9 years. The days on the market, the music festivals, that weird vertical dance tournament we catered in Hackney, the rooftops in Shoreditch, all the way to our lovely pizzerias. Thanks for eating our pizza. Maybe you even bought the book? Well actually, you would have had to, to be reading this… We're rambling… thank you.

Publishing Director
Sarah Lavelle

Editor
Harriet Webster

Copy Editor
Sally Somers

Head of Design
Claire Rochford

Art Direction and Design
Dave Brown

Photographer
Dave Brown

Head of Production
Stephen Lang

Production Controller
Katie Jarvis

First published in 2020 by Quadrille, an imprint of Hardie Grant Publishing

Quadrille
52–54 Southwark Street
London SE1 1UN
quadrille.com

Text © Pizza Pilgrims 2020
Photography © Dave Brown 2020
Design and layout © Quadrille 2020

Selected cover illustrations and half-title page © Ivana Zorn 2020 / pp.8–9 © Pizza Pilgrims Ltd 2020 / pp.12–13 © Pizza Pilgrims Ltd 2020 / p.14 background image: Urban Poster Mockup/Creative Market / p.19 top-right © David Tett Photography Ltd / pp.20–21 © Pizza Pilgrims Ltd 2020 / p.22 © Jason Bailey Studio 2018 / p.23 © Daniel Hambury, Stella Pictures Ltd 2020 / pp.30–31 Vegetables Engravings Set/Graphic Goods/Creative Market / p.31 Buffalo Illustrations © 1979 by Dover Publications, Inc. / p.33 Queen Margherita, credit: unknown / p.33 picture corners: Photo Corner and Frame/LiliGraphie/Creative Market / p.34 © Pizza Pilgrims Ltd 2020 / pp.38–41 creuxnoir 1044874746 / pp.42–45 background image: dikobraziy 515086592 / p.43 © Gino's East Ltd 2020 / pp.44–45 © Pizza Pilgrims Ltd 2020 / p.48 © David Tett Photography Ltd / p.50 bottom-left © Pizza Pilgrims Ltd 2020 / pp.54–55 background: Nicola Ferrari 1185515554 / p.55 Sophia Loren/GettyImages-78170723 Archive Photos/Stringer via Getty Images / p.71 background image © Pizza Pilgrims Ltd 2020 / pp.72,75,84–85 © Andy Rash 2020 / p.76 © Pizza Pilgrims Ltd 2020 / p.77 © Lateef Photography 2020 / p.95 © Pizza Pilgrims Ltd 2020 / p.101 © Pizza Pilgrims Ltd 2020 / pp.102–103 © Lateef Photography 2020 / p.170 © Pizza Pilgrims Ltd 2020 / p.178 © Mia Buerk, Papa Johns (GB) Ltd / p.181 background: Old homework papers/Paper Farms/Creative Market / p.185 © Pizza Pilgrims Ltd 2020 / p.190 © Pizza Pilgrims Ltd 2020 / p.193 top + middle © Pizza Pilgrims Ltd 2020 / pp.194–195 © Pizza Pilgrims Ltd 2020 / p.197 © Jens Hofma, PIZZA HUT RESTAURANTS UK® / pp.198–200 © Tobatron 2020 / p.202 © PIZZA HUT RESTAURANTS UK® / p.206 © Randy Duchaine 2020 / p.211 © Scott Bush, Domino's Pizza UK & Ireland Ltd 2020 / pp.226–229 Pizza Pattern/Ladies&co./Creative Market / p.245 © Robert Stanzione 2020 / p.256 © Pizza Pilgrims Ltd 2020 / pp.257–259 © Gino's East Ltd 2020

The publisher has made every effort to trace the copyright holders.
We apologize in advance for any unintentional omissions and would be pleased to insert the appropriate acknowledgement in any subsequent edition.

The rights of James Elliot and Thom Elliot to be identified as the author of this work have been asserted by her in accordance with the Copyright, Design and Patents Act 1988. Cataloguing in Publication Data: a catalogue record for this book is available from the British Library.

ISBN: 978 1 78713 515 4

Printed in China